Mightier than a lord

Iain Fraser Grigor

the Highland crofters'
struggle for the land

Published in Scotland in 1979 by Acair Limited, Cromwell Street Quay, Stornoway, Isle of Lewis.

ISBN 0 86152 030 0

© 1979. Iain Fraser Grigor

Designed by Mackay Design Associates Ltd.
Printed by Nevisprint Ltd., Fort William, Scotland

Is Treasa Tuath na Tighearna

Barvas
18 May 1980

To Ken, as advance reading for your
next visit

John Murray

Acknowledgements

Acknowledgement is due to the following for permission to reproduce photographs:

Deer-stalking; Carnish, North Uist; Crofter family at Poolewe; Crofter children at Poolewe; by courtesy of *Edinburgh City Libraries.*

Inveraray Castle; Bracara, Loch Morar; Beaufort Castle; Armadale Castle; Dunrobin Castle; Stornoway Castle; by courtesy of the *Royal Commission on Ancient Monuments, Scotland.*

John MacPherson; John MacPherson addresses a Land League Meeting; Sheriff Ivory etc; Marines land on Major Fraser's estate; Marines on the march; Dr. R. Macdonald; Mr J. MacDonald-Cameron; by courtesy of the *Illustrated London News.*

Post and Telegraph Office, Eriskay; Carsaig Bay; Tenants on Coll; Crofter's home, Stornoway; by courtesy of the *Highland Folk Museum, Kingussie.* Glen Tilt, Perthshire; by courtesy of the *National Museum of Antiquities, Scotland.*

10th Baron Napier; Drawing room of Mar Shooting Lodge; The 8th Duke of Argyll; John Stuart Blackie; The Marquis of Lorne; by courtesy of the *Scottish National Portrait Gallery.*

Moving furniture; Family with furniture; by courtesy of *Inverness Museum and Art Gallery.*

Big John Balachraggan reproduced by gracious permission of *Her Majesty the Queen.*

John Stewart of Valtos; by kind permission of *Donald Macleod, Achadhchorc.*

Contents

Introduction

'Woe unto them that join house to house,
that lay field to field,
till there be no place,
that they may be placed alone in the
midst of the earth!'

ISAIAH

In the year 1603, James VI of Scotland added to his titles that of James I of England; and the century was scarcely gone when the Parliaments of both countries were likewise merged to provide an adequate governing instrument for the united and increasingly great kingdom of Britain.

For the Scottish Parliament it was, as was said at the time, the 'end of ane auld sang', and for the English it was a fine success, a union—as was said later—suggestive of that which unites a small boy with an apple; while for the rich and the powerful, whether Scottish or English, it was merely another stepping-stone on the path to even greater riches and power. The Union brought together the landed and commercial interests of Scotland and England in the pursuit of a common interest; and the Union was to advance that interest in not a few ways—not least as a key factor in the emergence of what came to be known as the British Empire.

In all these developments, the common people were not consulted; for the common people, as such, had no concerted voice with which to speak. Popular insurrections there had been, over the centuries, but always in strictly local and limited contexts; in 1707, the forces which would later support the emergence of effective popular resistance to oppression were still dormant.

And of no area of Britain was this more true than of the Highlands of Scotland; indeed the very concept of popular political concern was quite irrelevant to the Highlands of the time. For in addition to the general considerations already noted, the Highlands had inherited attitudes going back to the rigidly aristocratic clan society of earlier centuries. At the same time, however, though the ordinary Highlander obeyed a strict code of loyalty and service to a local superior or clan chief (which made him an outstanding soldier in the British Army from the later eighteenth century onwards), he knew no such tradition of subservience to a distant, impersonal authority like central government. Moreover, a tradition of intermittent warfare, albeit on a small scale, was part of the not too distant past in most parts of the Highlands. Factors such as these had helped to create, in English and Lowland minds, an ill-defined but profound sense of unease about the Highlands—an insecurity which was both justified and reinforced by the Jacobite risings of 1715, 1719 and 1745.

In 1715 the cause of James, the Old Pretender, attracted the support of many Highland clans. The rising failed; and thirty years later, when his son Charles essayed a similar venture, this too ended in failure, with the destruction of Charles's Highland army on the bleak moor of Culloden. Then, while the Young Pretender took to his heels and to the hills, and soon enough to France, the British Government set about neutralising for ever the military potential of the Highlands, and cast about to find ways of undermining the cultural and social identity of the Highland people.

The next century and a half saw great changes in the Highlands. The remains of the clan system were finally dispersed by a combination of political and economic forces. The despised Highlanders, with their long record of insurrection, were now to be brought within the compass of southern authority, for a very powerful reason: a surplus of monetary wealth, generated by industrialisation, was now available for investment throughout the world, thereby to create even greater wealth and empire; but before this new era could safely be ushered in, it was necessary to ensure the quiescence of Britain's Highland backyard. It thus became an end of government policy to destroy the Highland threat to the new social order—to 'extirpate Celtic barbarism' and 'civilise' the Highlands, as they called it. And if, as they underwent this civilising process, the Highland land or people could be made to contribute to the 'common good', so much the better: for no two principles combined so harmoniously, to that progressive age, as those of profit and order. In the years from Culloden until the last quarter of the nineteenth century, the pursuit of profit and order was to underlie all change in the Highlands.

For the common people of the Highlands, of course, this policy and attitude had great and grave consequences, since they led directly to what are known now as the Highland Clearances—a time when, in the name of progress, and for the profit and pleasure of the few, men replaced men with sheep, and then (when sheep in their turn became a liability) turned the sheep-farms into deer-forests. In all this, of course, the opinions of those most affected, the ordinary people, were not sought; and any resistance on their part was for a long time inhibited—by the strength of their own traditional attitudes, and by the supreme confidence with which the doctrine of 'improvement' was presented and applied to them by authority in all its forms.

Then, in the 1880s, when the Highlands had long been thought 'pacified', there arose a movement of a quite revolutionary character, which challenged not only the authority of the southern legislature, but also the credentials of the Highland landowning elite, by calling in question the then-sacred principle that it was the task of the poor man to create wealth and the task of the rich man to spend it—the lot of the crofter to work the land and that of the landlord to enjoy its fruits. This movement brought a new self-awareness, solidarity and confidence to ordinary people, and created an active association of the crofting population throughout the Highlands in a very short space of time. It proposed changes which called in question the very basis of the Highland landlord—the right in law to own and dispose of land without reference to those who lived and worked upon it. In the course of the Highland land agitation, the law of the land, and especially the law relating to private landed property, was broken again and again. There were violent clashes between crofters and law-officers; there were confrontations involving gunboats, marine task-forces and military occupations; but the popular will could not be thwarted, and in the end the landlords and their forces were compelled to retreat and capitulate, in what has since become known as the Crofters' War.

This book tells the story of that war—of the land war and class war in the Highlands in the 1880s, and of the manner in which the crofting community secured a signal victory against the power, wealth and authority of the Highland landlords.

The seeds of revolt

*'The art of agriculture is no exception;
in it, as in all the others, the
accumulation of capital and the advance
of knowledge and of skill dispense with
half-employed and unproductive labour;
... a population numerous, but accustomed
to, and contented with, a low standard of
living for themselves, and yielding no
surplus for the support of others, gives
place to a population smaller in amount,
but enjoying a higher civilisation, and
contributing in a corresponding degree
to the general progress of the world.'*

THE DUKE OF ARGYLL

For the old Highland society, the short and bloody contest on Culloden Moor in April, 1746, was a cruel death-blow. By the end of that century, great changes had made themselves felt in the Highlands. Profit and order, the ideals of the new Establishment, were now the standards by which good and bad were to be judged in the Highlands. The former Jacobite chiefs and their forces no longer effectively existed. For their sons and grandsons, the choice was now one of oblivion, or the service of the new order. For the attainted Frasers of Lovat, and for many others, service in the armed forces of that new order was the route to survival. And as the old Highland aristocracy found a new role to play in the army and empire of the southern Establishment, so it was with the lesser men of the former clans. In 1813, for instance, Alex Morrison, the Kintail minister's son, died in Java; from Spain, it was reported that Lieutenant MacKenzie of Ross-shire had also fallen in the service of the Crown. On the bleak island of Heligoland, the tomb-stone of Lieutenant Gray from Inverness was under construction; Alexander Grant of Glenmoriston was dying in Canada; and on the last day of August, John Ross from Ross fell in arms at Mayo.

Meanwhile, on the home front, Glengarry was advertising great tracts of the former clan-lands for sale as sheep-farms, sheep being more fashionable and more profitable than human tenants. Many other landlords and former clan chiefs followed suit; and the people moved, or were moved, to the seashores, to the cities and to the far colonies. In April, 1821, seventy five years almost to the day since he had fought with the clans at Culloden, Alexander MacFarquhar died quietly in his native village; and within the decade, the chain of events set in motion by that confrontation would be entering its final phase. In the summer of 1828 a brig left Harris bound for Upper Canada, and two vessels left Lochmaddy crammed to the gunwales with 600 emigrants from North Uist. The following year there was a similar exodus from Skye to Cape Breton; and in 1830 nearly a thousand souls left the shores of Sutherland to journey to distant Canada. On the island of Rhum, 400 people were evicted to make room for one sheep-farmer and 8,000 sheep. Two years later the island of Muck was similarly 'improved'. By 1831 two-thirds of the inhabitants of the Uists and Benbecula were destitute, living on shell-fish and a broth made of sea-weed and nettles; and this was but a hint of things to come.

And while the people were impoverished—in the name of the prosperity of the Highlands—the great tide of sheep flooded north ever more strongly. In 1811 there were perhaps a quarter of a million sheep in the Highlands; by the 1840s they numbered close on a million; and that number continued to grow relentlessly. For a century after Culloden, three factors of change operated in the Highlands: the cultural conversion of the old élite; the disintegration of the traditional social framework of the common people; and the introduction of 'improving economics', as typified by the boom in sheep-farming. To these must be added a fourth and remarkable factor—the infrequency and ineffectiveness of popular resistance to these great changes, right through to the end of the 1840s.

Dunrobin Castle. 'It is the opinion of this country that should the Czar of Russia take possession of Dunrobin Castle and of Stafford House next term that we couldn't expect worse treatment at his hands than we have experienced at the hands of your family for the last fifty years'—unidentified speaker to the Duke of Sutherland, at Golspie.

That decade began with a continuation of the earlier pattern of eviction and destitution. Overt resistance was still absent, though the desertion of the Established Church for the new Free Church by the mass of the Highland people, after the great Disruption of 1843, clearly indicated a widespread dis-satisfaction with the way things were going in the Highlands. By that year, those who had not been forced to emigrate abroad or to the cities had been cleared to the margins of the land they and their fathers had once cultivated, and were there compelled by force of circumstances to subsist almost entirely on the potato, now the staple crop of the Highland population. When, in the mid 1840s, that crop failed, the people faced starvation. There were riots the length of the east coast, in Grantown-on-Spey, in Inverness, Evanton, Avoch, Beauly, Dingwall, Invergordon and Wick; on the west coast conditions were identical, save that there were no meal ships to attack. The Sheriff of Fort William, reporting on the hunger in Morar and Moidart and Arisaig, revealed that of the 900 people in Arisaig alone, 700 were dying of hunger; and matters were no different anywhere else in the Highlands.

The response of the landlords was less than benevolent; they complained bitterly at being required (as rate-payers) to spend some of their money to preserve a population which they now considered to be quite redundant. Where they were obliged to provide such support, they made sure that it was earned, by enforced labour at starvation wages. In Arisaig, for instance, the hungry were employed under the Drainage Act, which enabled men with families to earn just as much as would buy them meal for one week. 'They must sow as much barley as possible now that they have lost all hope of potatoes, on which I may say they heretofore entirely depended in this country', reported Donald MacCallum, the young and radical minister in the district. 'But how are they to sow their land? Seed will be high and scarce here, and most of the small tenants cannot obtain it. Lord Cranston is most desirous that all able-bodied men go south ...' In Sutherland, the Duke exacted work in return for bread, and his hungry were despatched to drain uncultivated land; while in winter he allowed soup to be made from hundreds of his red deer—a doubtful privilege when one considers that, out of season, their flesh would have been rancid and inedible to any but the starving.

Emigration, the landlords loudly cried, was the answer; and the Duke of Sutherland actually paid people to clear out to Canada. In three years, 1,000 people left the north-west of Sutherland alone, bound for Upper Canada and Cape Breton. Five shiploads of emigrants sailed from Laxford; though it cost the landlords £7,000 to send them, they though it money well-spent. In South Uist, the *Tusker* sailed from Lochboisdale for Quebec with five hundred emigrants; within weeks another 250 followed in her wake, facing a three months' voyage to make new homes on the far side of the Atlantic Ocean.

To those who remained the landlords recommended the virtue of sacrifice. As an example, the Lord Steward of the Queen's Household announced that Her Majesty, 'taking into consideration the increasing price of provisions, and especially of all kinds of bread and flour', had been graciously pleased to command that, beneath her palatial roofs, the daily allowance of bread be henceforth restricted to one pound per head for every person there billeted. Inspired by Her Majesty's example, four dukes and ten other peers of the realm pledged to reduce in their household—'as far as is practicable'—the consumption of bread and flour. At the Lord Mayor's feast in May, Lord John Russell discoursed on the moral value of eating less; and in the gay and splendid Stafford House in London, with its tartan-liveried footmen, the Duke of Sutherland devised and publicised his own sacrifice in support of the starving natives of the north: he pledged himself to eat not so much as one potato for as long as the famine might last.

Despite these minor privations, and the unsightly bother of hunger at the castle gates, being a Highland landowner had its compensations. For the Highland 'chief', and the romantic image of the Highlands, were coming to enjoy an increasingly glamorous status in the eyes of society at large. The Duke of Sutherland was transforming his Highland seat, Dunrobin Castle, into a 'princely residence'; the transformation took five years to complete, at enormous expense. Deer-stalking was growing in popularity; in Badenoch, of Cluny Macpherson's £2,000 rental, £1,360 came from his deer-forest alone. Prince Albert himself visited Inverness to attend the functions and grand balls of the Highland 'season', and later expressed himself much gratified with the romance and colour of the whole visit.

In August, 1847, the Queen and her party came to Loch Laggan for their holidays, the estate having been lent to them by its owner, the Marquis of Abercorn. They entertained themselves with the new fashion of Highland Games, and the children particularly enjoyed sailing in the barge that had been carried over the hills for the royal party, with its six sailors to row it, its handsome brass fittings and its tasselled silk canopy. Her Majesty planted two trees to commemorate her holiday in the romantic Highlands; and on her way back to London she visited Cluny Castle, where the tartan-clad chief had his son present the Prince of Wales with a ring containing a miniature portrait of Charles Edward Stuart, the Young Pretender—or Bonnie Prince Charlie, the Young Chevalier, as educated opinion now chose to remember him.

For some 'Highlanders', then, if not for the native Highland population, the 1840s had been a splendid time. But by the end of that decade one can discern the first signs of opposition to the 'improving' order in the Highlands. For some time past, Highland society had been resolving itself into a mass of impoverished and land-hungry crofters on the one hand, and an élite of wealthy and often absentee landlords on the other. It was inevitable that some day people would wake up to this fact. In 1847, the shoe-makers of Inverness formed a trade union, demanded better wages, and announced that they would no longer work with anyone who was not

The Highlander of Victorian romance.

John Grant and John Fraser—'Big John Balachraggan'—a tenant at Balachraggan, Beauly, near Brockie's Corner and Beaufort Castle. An uncle of the author's great-grandmother, he was sent in February, 1868, to Inverness 'to have dress prepared,' and then to Edinburgh for this portrait to be painted for a member of the Victorian aristocracy.

'When Lord Lovat was married, his coach was stopped at Brockie's Corner, and the horses unyoked, and Big John was invited to sit in the coach between Lord Lovat and his bride, and the coach was then drawn by clansmen unto the castle.'

also a member of their union. Four of their leaders were promptly arrested for breaking the law and challenging the rights of property and the liberty of enterprise. And two years later the people of Sollas in North Uist combined to challenge Lord MacDonald's rights of property, in the following manner.

Over the preceding half-century many Hebridean landlords had made fortunes from the kelp industry. By 1800, Lord MacDonald alone was getting £20,000 a year in income from his tenants' exertions on the sea-shores. The population was allowed to rise by the landlords, who also did their best to prevent emigration as long as it suited them, so that they could maximise their profit from the kelp. Landholdings were made smaller and smaller, and rents continually driven up, so that the people were forced to work at the kelp, and an abundance of labour allowed wages to be kept ridiculously low. With the collapse of the kelp industry however, the islands of the Hebrides were abandoned to the mercies of the southern property markets; and the new breed of Highland landlords had no use or desire for a native population encumbering their properties. In Skye, for instance, a thousand people were evicted or threatened with eviction every year for the next forty years; and elsewhere in the Highlands, the record was substantially similar.

Thus it was with Lord MacDonald in 1849. In that year he announced his intention to evict 600 people from Sollas and replace them with sheep. He offered to pay their way to Canada, and promised that, once they were safely there, he would not pursue them for any rent-arrears they might still owe on their crofts in distant Uist. The people, however, refused his Lordship's terms, and ignored the minister's insistent advice that they should accept them. For some months things dragged on, until in July MacDonald's factor brought the sheriff-substitute to Sollas to inform the natives that if they did not get out, they would be thrown out. The factor and the sheriff returned three times that month, with twenty constables, and each time they were turned back by a crowd of hundreds. Lord MacDonald asked for soldiers and bayonets; the authorities suggested that he should try once again with constables, and sent thirty-three of them to Sollas, along with the sheriff, the procurator-fiscal, a police superintend-ent, the minister, and MacDonald's factor.

The party marched into Sollas, and when the occupier of each house replied that he did not wish to go to Canada, or anywhere else for that matter, the police threw the poor furniture outside and set about tearing away the roof. After a violent riot, in which four prisoners were taken, the minister persuaded the people to renounce resistance, by asserting that if they did not, their houses would be torn to bits, and it would be wrong to resist that. In September, the four Sollas men appeared in court in Inverness, charged with mobbing, rioting, obstruction, and deforcement. Lord Cockburn, with all the sagacity of his many years on the Bench, observed to the jury that the matter had nothing to do with morality, 'with which you and I have no concern'; MacLean, Macphail, Boyd and

Between 1840 and 1883, decrees of eviction obtained against crofters in Skye alone involved a total of 83,000 people—Napier Report.

'The departure of the redundant part of the population is an indispensable preliminary to every kind of improvement...'; the *Economist*, speaking of crofters rather than landlords.

20

MacCuish were then found guilty and given four months each. Four years later, on Boxing Day, 1853, the people of Sollas finally embarked from Campbeltown on the *Captain Baynton*, bound for the colonies. Apart from such very minor upsets, nothing seemed likely to challenge the unlimited freedom of action of the Highland landlords. Such, indeed, was their collective sense of security that, during the week when the Sollas men were sentenced, the main focus of interest in polite Highland circles was the construction of a memorial cairn on Culloden Moor — for Culloden was a part of the romantic Jacobite myth then in vogue — rather than anything to do with crofter intransigence.

The year 1850 in the Highlands saw the Queen come to Balmoral, and Lord Ashley holiday with the Sutherlands in Dunrobin. Lord and Lady Gough, lately returned from India, holidayed in Glen Urquhart, and enjoyed the 'well-attended and brilliant' Northern Meeting Ball in Inverness. In July, the London Highland Fete was equally brilliant, with the aristocracy resplendent in what was coming to be called 'Highland costume'. In the same year John Macdonnell of Keppoch, whose grandfather had died in the heather at Culloden, passed away at the age of 84; he was the last Highlander, it was said, who had actually seen the Young Pretender — in later years when the Prince had abandoned his pretensions and settled forever in European exile.

It was to be a decade of further destitution and forced emigration. There were four thousand destitute in the western parishes of Kilmallie and Ardnamurchan and Glenelg. The Duke of Sutherland paid some more of his natives to leave Scrabster for Quebec. In Lewis, Sir James Matheson paid the fares of a thousand emigrants from Loch Roag to the far colonies. In Barra and South Uist, Colonel Gordon had four ships transport five hundred islanders from the former and a thousand from the latter. Four hundred families from Skye were offered a free passage, if they would only agree to be sent to Australia. The Government made available seven ships from London and eight from Birkenhead for 'approved Highland emigrants'. At the end of 1852, four hundred people from Skye arrived in Birkenhead on their way to Australia. In October, a hundred Lochaber people sailed for the Antipodes, their former landlord, Lochiel, having promised not to pursue them for rent-arrears once they were safely there. While these events were taking place, Lord Orkney appeared at the Ball of the Emperor of France wearing highly-fashionable Highland costume: '... the knife at the garter, the hunting horn, the plaid, the kilt, the bonnet, the sporran, all complete'. This outfit, it was reported, attracted much attention. At the Great Exhibition in London, the Highland Stall, 'surmounted by a splendid deer's head, with two eagles on the side pillars, ... with its tartans, brooches, cairngorms and tweeds made a brave show'.

In October 1851 Patrick Sellar, the Duke of Sutherland's infamous sheep-farmer, died at last; but the 'improving' process in the Highlands, with which he had for so long and so profitably been associated, went on apace. The previous year a new sheep-farmer had attempted to evict 620 people from his estate at Strathaird in Skye. He offered to pay their way to Canada; and, by way of further inducement, threatened to hasten them on their way by calling on the military. They were also informed that though they might starve, they would get no further assistance from the Relief Board. In the spring of 1852, the Marquis of Stafford informed forty of his tenants at Coigach, Loch Broom, that he required them out, as their land was to be put under sheep. The people threatened deforcement; the Lord Advocate was asked for soldiers; and in the meantime a party of sheriff-officers was deforced, and their writs of removal were burned before them.

Fearing serious violence, the Marquis withdrew his eviction plans. The following year there was more trouble in Skye. In one small community, thirty-two families were given notice to quit in the spring; and in September the estate factor, who was also the local sheriff-officer, began to eject the people. There was a violent fight, and three prisoners were taken —John and Duncan Macrae and Sandy MacInnes. Later, in Inverness, they were found guilty of deforcement. They returned home; and at Christmas the factor came again and turned everyone out, men, women, and children, in the bitter cold of the winter. By the following spring, there were still twenty of them surviving on the shore and the hill; in January a statement on behalf of the landlord explained that he had been over-indulgent with his tenants.

Soon afterwards there was further trouble in the east; and again the law and the forces of the law were to remind the labouring population of its responsibilities with respect to private property. Close to Bonar Bridge, writs of removal were issued against a community of four hundred people; but the sheriff-officer who was to serve them was deforced, stripped naked, and his writs were burned. On the last day of March, 1854, the sheriff returned with forty police officers, only to be met by a crowd three hundred strong. A violent conflict ensued, in which twenty women were seriously injured by the police batons; this was neither the first nor the last time in the history of resistance to landlordism that the womenfolk of a community took the lead. That day by Bonar Bridge four women were taken prisoner—two Margarets, a Chrissy, and an Ann, all surnamed Ross. On 12 April the law selected Ann Ross to be tried in court; since a male ringleader was also needed, for the sake of appearances, it was decided that one Peter Ross should be tried along with her. They appeared in court in Inverness in September, accused of mobbing and rioting, breach of the peace, and assault on police-officers; induced to plead guilty to breach of the peace, they were sentenced to twelve months and eighteen months of hard labour respectively. Lord Justice Clerk Hope, who had spent his summer recess pursuing game over the desolation of his son's estate in Sutherland, opined that the defendants and their like could not be allowed to live in a wicked and rebellious spirit against the law, and reminded the jury that there existed a 'singular and perverted feeling of insubordination' in some districts of the Highlands; 'this feeling is most prejudicial to the interests of all and it is absolutely necessary to suppress it'. So Ann and Peter Ross were sentenced and taken away; and their having pled guilty meant that the death of Margaret Ross of Greenyards, resulting from the blows of police batons, was not brought before the court or the public gaze.

The Lord Justice Clerk had announced that the people had to be taught submission in the very first instance; and in Knoydart, in western Inverness-shire, the people were to pay in full the price of such submission. In 1853 the trustees of MacDonnell of Glengarry decided to evict several hundreds of their tenants, and let their land to a sheep-farmer. Over three hundred of the people agreed to go voluntarily to Canada, and as they left, their houses were promptly destroyed, to encourage the others to go away too. Some did not go; but a few weeks after the three hundred had sailed, the houses of those who had stayed behind were torn stone from stone, their inhabitants were driven forth with axe and crowbar, and sheep came on the hill. Thirty of those people lived for a time in the ruins of their former homes, but their shelters and huts were continually destroyed by the estate authorities; and by 1855 they too had gone, leaving Knoydart desolate and empty.

In June of that same year James Loch, the great 'improving' agent of the Duke of Sutherland's estates, became ill in London while attending the visit of the Emperor of France. On the twenty-eighth day of the month the most hated man in Sutherland died. Joseph Mitchell was travelling in the county at that very time, and many years later he was to write that, 'along the whole course of my journey through the county, I was asked in quiet, exulting whispers, "Did you hear the news? Loch is dead!"'.' In his time as factor Loch had seen, and assisted in, the near-extirpation of a society, a culture, and a people. During those years his work had met with little resistance; and for twenty years after his death 'the struggles of advancing civilisation' (as they were once described in the drawing-room of Dunrobin Castle) had not been complicated by crofter intransigence, except in a fitful and unco-ordinated way. The Rev. Thomas MacLauchlan of the Free Gaelic Church put it in different terms; 'There is a fierce and un-natural struggle commenced between capital and population, and it is not difficult to predict that the former will be the winning party'. But then, in 1874, events occurred which clearly gave notice of changed days to come.

In the island of Lewis, the man with the capital was Sir James Matheson of Stornoway Castle. He had extensive interests in the Far East; but tiring of commerce, and having accumulated an immense fortune, he had returned to Britain and a suitably eminent place in society. Soon owner of the estate of Lewis and its surrounding islands, he was elected Member of Parliament for Ross-shire by his fellow landlords. During the potato famine he spent £60,000 refurbishing Stornoway Castle as his Highland seat, and was created a baronet for his 'untiring benevolence in relieving the inhabitants of Lewis during the famine'. As a matter of fact, Sir James, part of whose fortune was requisitioned to prevent widespread starvation, disapproved strongly of what he called the lavish waste of money in the

Sir James Matheson's castle in Stornoway, built with the profits of the China opium trade. In *Sybil*, Disraeli referred to Matheson as '...a dreadful man, richer than Croesus, one McDrug, fresh from Canton with a million of opium in each pocket'.

Crofting tenants of Sir James Matheson, near Stornoway.

Government's famine-relief programme. He thought it better for the poor people to labour for their means of sustenance—'that they ought rather to earn their food by toil, than eat the bread of idleness and pauperism'—and so set his own tenants to work on his estate for just enough food to keep them alive and working. Perhaps his eastern experiences helped him to balance this delicate equation: for the greatest portion of his truly huge fortune had been made in the China opium addiction trade, which he had once recommended to a friend as 'the safest and most gentlemanlike speculation I am aware of'.

Matheson was a man well-used to absolute authority, and was certainly not accustomed to opposition of any significance from the common people with whom his little empire brought him into contact. But in the year 1874 Sir James's crofting tenants on the island of Bernera, off the west side of Lewis, were finally to challenge their landlord's despotism. It was Matheson's factor, Munro, who dispensed that great power, and factor Munro's jurisdiction was severely exercised. Fines and threats of eviction followed any crofter who chose to appear before him wearing a cap or with his hands in his pockets, or in an insufficiently deferent manner; for years, such petty intimidation had been typical of social relations on the Matheson estate. But in March, 1874, the deference and quiescence of the Bernera crofters gave way to organised and determined resistance. It began when summonses were served on fifty-six crofters, instructing them and their families 'to remove from the acres, garden, grass and houses' of the over-crowded and over-rented island, together with their grazing-ground in Earshader on the nearby mainland of Lewis. The reception they gave to sheriff-officer Maclellan the day he called to deliver these writs was far from deferential, and resulted, four months later, in a court case long remembered in the island of Lewis.

On the morning of 17 July 1874, in the Sheriff Criminal Court in Stornoway, Angus Macdonald, Norman Macaulay and John Macleod, all of Bernera, were charged with having 'wickedly and feloniously' assaulted Maclellan, of having pulled and jostled him, and of having threatened to kill him, 'by all which Colin Maclellan was put into a state of great terror and alarm, and was injured in his person'.

They pled not guilty, a jury was sworn in, and the trial commenced. The factor himself was the first witness to be called for the prosecution. An Inverness solicitor, Innes, representing the accused, examined Munro relentlessly, to the delight of the packed public gallery. The factor began by complaining of how until recenly he had been procurator-fiscal in Lewis, and of how the Sheriff of Ross, Cromarty and Sutherland had withdrawn his commission as the chief law-officer in the island as a result of the proceedings now in hand. He did not think that there was any reason why he should not be both factor and procurator in Lewis; from the Bench, Sheriff Fordyce's substitute, Charles Spittal, listened intently, but made no comment. Munro then had difficulty remembering all his posts in the administration of Lewis, and could not confirm that he held, or did not hold, some of them; the defence agent assured the court of all his many interests and posts. Munro told the court that though the summonses of removal of March had said that the Bernera crofters were to be cleared off both their grazing-land on Lewis and their own little island, he had only intended that they leave their Lewis grazing-land. He did not know how many crofters were to be removed—such details, he explained, were left to his subordinates, as he was a busy man; and, he angrily objected, what business had the court to be asking questions like this anyway? He had spared his valuable time to convict crofters of assault, not to discuss the private matters of Sir James's private property. The sheriff-substitute leaned forward at that, across the exhibits lying in the well of the court, and observed that Mr Munro would be well-advised to answer such questions as were put to him. Twice, Munro refused to confirm that it had been his intention to clear the Bernera people altogether; when the summonses of removal were read to the court, he retorted with annoyance, 'I obtained decree on the summonses of removing, and if I wished it I could have removed all the tenants from their crofts and houses in Bernera, as well as from the summer grazings in Lewis, because the decrees gave me the power to do so'. Which was one way of saying, perhaps, that he had been doing what he liked for twenty years, and did not see why he should not go on in that way. As for the fifty-six families to be evicted, he had not consulted Sir James Matheson about removing the people, and had issued all the summonses of removing against them without receiving instructions from him to do so. 'I am not in the habit of consulting Sir James,' said Munro, 'about every little detail connected with the management of the estate'. The defence lawyer asked Munro whether it was true that when the Bernera people had got the Earshader grazing-ground, he had promised them that they would have it as long as they were living on Bernera. The factor could not remember. Was it true that he had actually signed a document promising this? He could not remember that either. Had not such a document been prepared in his office and sent out with a deputy who was to read it out to the crofters and get them to sign it, and had it not been signed and returned to him? Again, Munro could not remember. It was true, however, that before the estate had rented the people of Bernera the Earshader grazing-ground, they had occupied a much better piece of land immediately adjoining Earshader. From this they had been removed, so that it could be made into a deer-forest for Sir James and his guests.

When their grazings had been moved to Earshader, the people of Bernera had built a seven-mile dry-stone dyke to protect their land from the deer of the newly-created deer-forest. Innes next asked Munro whether grazing and dyke were now being taken from them with no compensation for the dyke they had built at their own expense. Munro retorted that they had never been promised any compensation. He agreed that it had been his policy to overcrowd the people on Bernera by the expedient of refusing them the use of Sir James's ferry boat from the island to Lewis. This was simply for their own good: 'I considered the confining of the crofters to the

26

island of Bernera was safer for them, their families and cattle, because they would have to cross the ferry, which in my opinion was dangerous'. He did not explain, however, why it was that, though Sir James's millions could buy the 250-ton *Marquis of Stafford* as his private yacht, they could not buy a ferry fit to cross a matter of yards of enclosed water.

Munro told the court that when he had disallowed the Bernera men the use of the ferry and threatened to enforce the ruling with the Volunteer Militia, he had 'simply been joking'. He also explained how he had lately introduced a new form of arbitration in disputes between himself and the tenants: any disagreements were to be considered by three independent arbiters—all three being chosen, independently, by himself. Under cross-examination, the factor then revealed his special mechanism for the encouragement of emigration. If one impoverished family was evicted for arrears of rent, then no other family, whatever their circumstances, would get that land unless they paid Sir James the outstanding rent owed by the previous tenant. Moreover, as he came to the end of his evidence, Munro admitted that it was his policy to fine crofters whose stock wandered into the good land of the deer-forest; and that failure to pay the fine resulted in confiscation and eviction.

Munro stood down. The next witness for the prosecution was Colin Maclellan, Munro's sheriff-officer, who proceeded to give the court his version of what had happened in Bernera four months previously. He had gone over with Macrae, Munro's deputy, and Bain, the exciseman. At Breaclete and two other townships he had served summonses without trouble; but leaving Tobson that evening, his business concluded, he had been pursued by a crowd of men and women throwing stones and clods of earth. He had taken shelter that night, and was not interrupted; and in the morning walked to Breaclete to be collected by boat. On the way there, however, a party of men accosted him, among them the three men now standing before him in the dock. They informed him that they believed they had a right to the land they worked, threatened to drive him from the island naked, and forced him to promise never to return to Bernera, nor to tell anyone of what happened.

He concluded his statement. There was a stir in the packed chamber as a court-officer held up to view a dark top-coat, slightly torn, and some pieces of waterproof fabric, which the sheriff-officer identified as his top-coat and the remains of his waterproof coat—both damaged, he claimed, in the struggle with the accused. The agent for the crofters suggested that Maclellan, who served under the factor in the Volunteers, had threatened the Bernera people with a rifle. He did not deny this; but he could not remember saying that he looked with contempt on the powers of resistance of the Bernera men.

James Macrae, the factor's deputy with responsibility for Bernera, took the stand next. He confirmed Maclellan's testimony, and also confirmed that Sir James himself had refused the crofters' petition against eviction from their land. Macrae had been the local ground officer for five years, and he affirmed that when the Bernera grazings on Lewis had been moved to Earshader, to make way for the deer-forest, a document *had* been signed confirming that the people could thereafter keep Earshader as long as they stayed on Bernera. In this Macrae bluntly contradicted Munro. He stated too that before they commenced building the seven mile long stone wall on Earshader, which required many thousands of tons of heavy stone to be quarried and carted by hand, the Bernera people had received assurances that they would not be evicted in the future; and he concluded by assuring the court that in his recollection, Maclellan had said at the time of the alleged assault that he wished he had a firearm with him.

After Macrae, three more witnesses for the prosecution appeared, and contented themselves and the court with descriptions of what had happened when Maclellan and his party had visited the island. The case for the prosecution being concluded, the agent for the crofters intimated that he now wished to call witnesses—five Bernera men, four MacDonalds and a MacLeod, who were examined in Gaelic with the keeper of Stornoway gaol acting as interpreter. This evidence added little to what the jury had already heard; the defence lawyer then addressed the jury; and late in the evening sheriff-substitute Spittal delivered his summing-up and asked the jury to consider their verdict. So packed was the court that the jury could not retire; they conferred for a moment, and then indicated their verdict—'not guilty'. And as the three Bernera men walked free among the jubilant crowd outside the court, under the pale light of that summer night, they were, albeit unwittingly, the first real contestants and victors in the Highland land agitation. For at last the landowners and their agents had been challenged in their own courts of law, and had been defeated. Though the case that day had formally concerned assault, what had really been on trial was the management of the Lewis estate. Evidence relating to that management, though perhaps strictly irrelevant in terms of the rules of evidence to the charge of assault, had been skilfully introduced by the defence and permitted by the sheriff-substitute, with great results for the crofters.

The following morning John Smith, a baker in Stornoway, appeared in court charged with having attempted to rescue one of the Bernera men at the time of his arrest. Smith was dismissed from court; and shortly afterwards, Colin Maclellan himself was in court, charged with having assaulted in custody one of the Bernera defendants. He was found guilty and fined, with the alternative of imprisonment. Munro shortly relinquished his post as factor for the Matheson estate; and though the summonses of removal on the Bernera tenants were still valid and lawful, they were never again served, and the people of Bernera continued to graze their stock on the land of Earshader. It had been a famous victory for the people of Bernera, but it also marked a turning-point; for it can be seen now as the opening shot in the Highland crofters' offensive against the power and privilege and wealth of the Highland landlords. For the first time, in that fierce struggle of which Thomas MacLauchlan had written, population had decisively overcome capital; and this victory was soon to have repercussions across the length and breadth of the Highlands.

Sedition in the west

'No doubt there were improvements
of various kinds ... but the people
who were shovelled down to the
sea coast were not improved; and
it was not for their improvement
in any shape that the new roads
were made or the new bridges
constructed ... It was not the happiness
of the great mass of the people, but
the hasty enrichment of the few, that
was the alpha and the omega of their
economic gospel in the Highlands.'

JOHN STUART BLACKIE

In Britain as a whole the 1870s were years of social restiveness and change, and what happened on Sir James Matheson's estate in 1874 mirrored, in its own way, the experience of the country as a whole. For in the wider context, too, established social and political beliefs were being questioned in a way that had far-reaching implications for British society. The 'Irish Question' was ever to the fore, and in the manufacturing districts of the south the growing trade-union movement was increasingly demanding a share in the wealth which the industrial workforce created at such a terrible cost in human suffering. The 'two nations' of mid-Victorian Scotland were becoming starkly polarised; and in the Highlands, on the periphery of British economic and political life, those 'two nations' of rich and poor were as much in evidence as in the rest of the country. Industrial growth in the south was accompanied by the development of transport and communications in the Highlands. The railway came to Strome Ferry in 1870; and by 1880 Oban was linked by rail with the south. Where previously it could take a week to reach parts of the Highlands from Edinburgh, the railways and the telegraph now carried news and newspapers north in a fraction of that time. The telegraph offices, indeed, were soon to be the crofters' lifeline to their southern supporters, spokesmen and informants, and were destined to play a crucial part in the co-ordination of the coming agitation. Off the west coast, where a few years before only local fishing craft and the occasional trader under sail had plied, Matheson's *Marquis of Stafford* was joined by the vessels of the new coastal steamer service. By the end of the decade, indeed,

Eriskay's post and telegraph office in later years. These offices were the crofters' lifeline to their southern supporters and spokesmen.

communications had grown to such an extent that a copy of the Irish Land Bill was sent, hot from the press, to a crofter on the island of Lewis—or so it was reported by alarmed police sources to the Secretary of State.

Inspired in part, no doubt, by developments in the south, and facilitated by improved communications and transport in the Highlands, resistance to landlordism increased throughout the 1870s. There was plenty to resist: during the course of the decade, for instance, sixty writs of removal were issued each year against crofters in Skye alone. The power of the landlord and his factor was still largely unchallenged; with the threat of eviction ready to hand, the landlord possessed—and often exercised—a most formidable authority. In 1872, Roderick Macintosh of Skibo was evicted, along with his family, because his sons had poached salmon from the river that ran past his croft. Such fish, he was reminded, were private property, and protected by the full majesty of the law and landlord authority for the pleasure of the leisured—and most certainly not for consumption by the poor. Between 1840 and 1883 thirty-five thousand people on the island of Skye were subject to decrees of eviction. Nor did Parliament offer the crofters any remedy; for as late as the election of 1880 the restricted franchise meant that it was landlords who represented them in the Commons—merely complementing their brethren who sat in the House of Lords. For Inverness-shire the Member of Parliament returned in 1880 was Cameron of Lochiel, who owned 130,000 acres; for Caithness, Sinclair of Ulbster with 80,000 acres; for Ross-shire, Alexander Matheson, who had almost a quarter of a million acres; for Sutherland, the Marquis of Stafford, heir to the Duke of Sutherland with more than a million acres; and for Argyll, young Lord Colin, son of the Duke and heir to his acres. Argyll himself was shortly to write to Gladstone to say of the crofting communities in his own territory that, 'fortunately', there were now very few of them left. They were now living on what the Duke described as 'charity'; and he hoped that, 'not even the desire for social peace at any price will induce reasonable men to desire a return to a condition of things from which they have happily escaped'.

In the towns and cities of Scotland there were many people of Highland origin who would not have described their present existence as in any way the result of a 'happy escape'. Although their own connection with the Highlands had been severed, they did not forget their past; and as the 1870s advanced, that part of the Lowland population which was of Highland origin became increasingly active in the cause of the remaining Highland people. In conjunction with the growth of native resistance over the decade, this was to have spectacular results. As urban radicalism increased and as the Irish peasants' agitation grew more pressing, the matter of Highland land ownership became one of growing importance in political debate. The spirit of reform was in the air, and radical proposals on land use and ownership were increasingly aired. These were quickly taken up by the Highland groups in the southern towns and cities, by the Gaelic-speaking congregations and the many Highland and Celtic societies in

Glasgow, London, Edinburgh, Greenock, and even Birmingham; and in November, 1878, at a delegate meeting in Glasgow, they came together to form the Federation of Celtic Societies. The delegate from the Gaelic Society of Inverness, Alexander Mackenzie, proposed that the objects of the Federation should be the preservation of the Gaelic language and literature, the encouragement of Celtic education in schools and colleges, and generally the promotion of the interests of the Highlanders. Colin Chisholm of London, supporting Mackenzie, described the Highlands as hundreds of square miles converted into forests for wild beasts, while men and women, born and reared on these lands, were swept away and heaped together in the large towns, 'in layers almost as thick as herrings in a barrel'; it was terrible to see so much of the best grazing and arable land throughout the Highlands cut off from the use of man, while the deer-forests grew wider every year, and the space allotted for human beings was yearly curtailed. Mackenzie, who had been brought up on a Ross-shire croft until his father's eviction, was elected secretary to the Federation; his was to be a powerful voice in crofting affairs in the coming decade. And to it were added the organisational and rhetorical powers of two other office-bearers of the Inverness Gaelic Society, John Murdoch and John Stuart Blackie. Murdoch had been brought up on Islay, and possessed a fierce and unremitting hatred of Highland landlordism; he was to devote the following years to defending and advancing the cause of the common people of Highland Scotland. Blackie was Professor of Greek at Edinburgh University, where he played a large part in the establishment of the Chair of Celtic. Despite his pre-industrial and sometimes sentimental view of the Highlands, his dedicated defence of crofters against landlords, and his enduring championship of all things Celtic, ensured for him an important place in the movement.

In the forefront of the campaign were many with direct experience of life in the Highlands. Donald MacFarlane, the anti-landlord Irish Member of Parliament for County Carlow, had been born in Caithness, and had emigrated to Australia with his parents at the age of eight; in later years he was to emerge as a leading parliamentary representative of the Highland crofters, whose cause he was to adopt at the expense of his Irish interests. John Mackay, the president of the Glasgow Sutherland Association, to whom Mackenzie later dedicated his great history of the Clearances, had also been raised on a croft, in Sutherland; his money, which he had earned as a railway engineer in the south, helped to finance much pro-crofter activity. Roderick Macdonald, shortly to become president of the Gaelic Society of London, was born on a croft in Skye. At the meeting at which the Federation of Celtic Societies had been formed, one of the representatives of the Glasgow Sutherland Association was its secretary (and later president), Angus Sutherland; a young teacher at Glasgow Academy, his family had been evicted from their croft at Kildonan. Another committee member of the Glasgow Sutherland Association, also present at the founding meeting of the Federation, was John G Mackay, a

Glasgow draper, representing the Gaelic Society of Glasgow; his mother came from the cleared parish of Bracadale in Skye.

Another pillar of the Gaelic Society of Inverness was Charles Fraser-Mackintosh, Member of Parliament for Inverness Burghs. No crofter's son himself, Fraser-Mackintosh campaigned tirelessly with Blackie for the establishment of a Chair of Celtic at Edinburgh and for the extension of the teaching of Gaelic in Highland schools, where, at the time, instruction was conducted in English by Act of Parliament.

Between them, these men played a leading role in the 1870s in publicising the cause of the Highland crofters. Blackie, Mackenzie and Fraser-Mackintosh campaigned for the Gaelic language and Gaelic education. In 1873, Murdoch began to publish his newspaper, *The Highlander*, using it to encourage Gaelic and to agitate for a Highland land settlement that would give justice to the crofters. Publication ceased in 1881, as a result of a successful lawsuit brought by a Skye landlord whose mansion had been destroyed in a flood; *The Highlander* had suggested that this mishap was divine retribution for the landlord's rack-renting of his tenantry. In 1876, Mackenzie began to publish his *Celtic Magazine*, dedicated to the 'social and material interests of the Celt at home and abroad'. He despatched copies of his article, 'The Poetry and Prose of a Highland Croft', which was, in effect, a scathing denunciation of Highland landlordism, both to the Prime Minister and to the Duke of Argyll. Gladstone ignored it; Argyll replied that only by eviction would 'families who cling tenaciously to their traditional habits' be made fit to take a permanent place in the agricultural system of the country. Nevertheless, the subject was taken up by *The Inverness Courier* and by Murdoch's *Highlander*; the article was referred to widely and quoted extensively in many British newspapers; *The Scotsman* devoted two editorials to the topic, and despatched a special correspondent to the Highlands. The *Oban Times* was at this time rapidly turning into a radical and outspoken advocate of the crofters' cause. The *North British Daily Mail* also began to highlight the crofters' case. Towards the end of the decade, Mackenzie published a highly successful pamphlet on the Clearances; and Blackie delivered to the Perth Gaelic Society his influential address on 'Gaelic Societies, Highland Depopulation and Land Law Reform'. Mackenzie was agitating for Government action to save the remaining Highland population, and the Gaelic Society of Inverness petitioned Parliament likewise. Charles Cameron, owner of the *North British Daily Mail*, was also a Glasgow Member of Parliament; he and MacFarlane and Fraser-Mackintosh, and the pro-Highland Irish members, represented the nucleus of a parliamentary grouping in the crofter interest. Thus, by the end of the decade, the political infrastructure for a crofter's movement was in existence, with an organisation, sympathetic newspapers, parliamentary spokesmen, gifted and dedicated agitators, a massive reservoir of latent sympathy and support among working-class Highland expatriates, and the ever-present example of the Irish peasants' land agitation. And as the 1870s passed, there came a stepping-up of agitation and anti-landlord activities amongst the Highland crofters themselves.

On the last day of September 1873, widow MacFarlane of Tiree was found guilty of assault at Tobermory Sheriff Court; the previous month, she had used fire-tongs to defend her home against eviction, and in the process injured one of her evictors. That same year, the owner of Tiree, the Duke of Argyll, announced his intention of turning the people out of Glen Aray and making it into a deer-forest. There was little remarkable in either event; they were, indeed, characteristic of the tenor of Highland affairs up to that time; but towards the end of the same decade trouble of a new and challenging kind erupted on the Isle of Skye, in the district of Kilmuir. In the 1840s the minister of Kilmuir had written that the population of his parish was then four thousand souls. Of these, upwards of two thousand had no land from the proprietor. They had indeed small patches for planting potatoes; but that year these patches had yielded no return whatever, and they were now reduced to a state of abject famine. Neither would the remaining food resources in the district be able to afford them support for more than a month to come. 'In a short time, therefore, the whole population will become the victims of scarcity and famine', warned the minister; and in the succeeding decades, scarcity and hunger were no strangers to the people of Kilmuir.

By the end of the 1870s, indeed, there had been little improvement in conditions in Kilmuir. The proprietor was William Fraser, a leading figure in landlord circles, and a keen anti-crofter. He had increased rents in the 1850s and again in 1876-77, and had imposed other punitive charges on his impoverished tenantry. In 1881, perhaps encouraged by the growing support in the south, some of his tenants at Valtos defiantly refused to pay the increased rents. Fraser was able to force the closure of Murdoch's *Highlander* that year; but his threats of eviction against those who would not pay the new rents were simply ignored by the crofters of Valtos; and he backed down before the threat of his tenants' rent-strike. This small victory was to have significant effects.

In Ross-shire, in the parish of Lochbroom, there was trouble on the small estate of Leckmelm; from that trouble too, there were to be important results. In 1879, Colonel Davidson sold the estate to a city manufacturer named Pirie, who at once instructed his factor to inform the tenantry that the present arrangements by which they held their cottages, byres, and other buildings, together with land on the estate, would cease after the term of Martinmas, 1880; further, the factor was instructed to intimate that, at Martinmas, Pirie intended taking for himself *all* the arable and pasture land; and that unless the tenants at once prevented their stock from grazing on the land already in the possession of Pirie, 'he will not, upon any conditions, permit you to remain in the cottage you now occupy, after the said term of Martinmas 1880, but will clear all of the estate, and take down the cottages'.

Pirie's ultimatum affected in total twenty-three families, crofters who had tended their land until it was the best in the district. This land Pirie wanted for himself; and at Martinmas, 1880, he simply took it, and reduced the former crofters to cottars and day-labourers; though they were allowed to remain in their cottages, it was on the condition that they kept around them not so much as a dog. In one stroke, therefore, they were reduced from a position of relative poverty to a position of absolute poverty. And, despite widespread and largely hostile press comment, Pirie was not dissuaded from his course. His actions were, in the long run, to rebound badly on the Highland landlords.

When the eviction notices were served in Leckmelm, a local minister, John MacMillan, at once began an agitation against the activities of the new landlord. At the end of 1880, he appeared on the stage of the Music Hall in Inverness, to address a meeting of crofters' supporters. He spoke of recent events in Leckmelm, described Pirie's strategy for 'improvement' and told how, 'to strike terror into their hearts, first of all, two houses were pulled down, I might say about the ears of their respective occupants, without any warning whatsoever, except a verbal one of the shortest kind'. The first house was the home of a pauper woman, deaf and aged, who had lived alone for years in a cottage of her own, altogether apart from the other houses. After this eviction no provision was made for her by her new landlord, and she was left to get shelter elsewhere or anywhere, as best she could. The second tenant evicted by Pirie was a widow with two children; after the death of her husband she had tried to support herself and them by working in the house of a rich family as a servant, and it was from that family she had returned to Leckmelm, in failing health. Her father had died while she was away, and the house in which he lived and died, and in which she was born and bred, was now empty, with the land attached to it in the hands of another tenant. There, said MacMillan, 'she turned aside for a while until something else would in kind providence turn up. But behold during her sojourn from her native township, the inexorable edict had gone forth to raze her habitation to the ground. Her house also was pulled down about her ears. This woman has since gone to America ...'

The minister's speech was a long one; not only did he catalogue events in Leckmelm, but he offered a perceptive analysis of the mechanics of Highland landlordism. He dealt comprehensively with the matter of the Clearances; and, unlike so many of his kind, he condemned the things which were even then happening in the Highlands. At that meeting in the Music Hall, MacMillan explained that, since the time of the Clearances, things had changed very little for the Highland crofter, and explained how some landlords who had the name of being good and kind to their tenants, and who could not be charged with evicting any of them, were nevertheless inch by inch secretly and stealthily laying waste the country and undermining the position of the native people. For though when they took possession of their estates all promised fair and well, 'by and by the fatal blow was struck to dispossess the people'.

To be sure, none could now be forcibly burned out from their holdings;

that would be highly impolitic, because it would bring public condemn-ation on the landlords, and might stimulate support for the nascent popular resistance to landlord oppression. But in covert ways clearing still went on. When a tenant died, or removed otherwise, the order went forth that his croft was not to be worked again, whether by a neighbouring tenant or by a stranger. In this 'inch by inch' way the work of depopulation could be effected in a few years, or in a generation at most, quite as effectually as by the more glaring and obvious methods. This secret and insinuating way of depopulating the land should be stoutly resisted, MacMillan told his audience. 'What have these people done when they were so remorselessly driven from their native shores, year by year in batches of thousands?' Yearly, they had sent forth their thousands to follow the battle flag of the Empire. It had been a Highland defence that followed the broken wreck of Cumberland's army after the disastrous day at Fontenoy when more British soldiers lay dead upon the field than fell at Waterloo itself. It was another Highland regiment that scaled the rock-face over the St. Lawrence, 'and first formed a line in the September dawn on the level sward of Abraham'. It was a Highland line that broke the power of the Maharatta hordes and gave Wellington his maiden victory at Assaye. 'Thirty four battalions marched from these glens to fight in America, and in Germany, and India ere the 18th century had run its course'; and yet, while abroad over the earth, and always the first in assault and the last in retreat, 'their lowly homes in far-away glens were being dragged down, and the wail of women and the cry of children went out ... To convert the Highland glens into vast wastes untenanted by human beings—such was the work of laws formed in a cruel mockery of name by the Commons of England.'

MacMillan's analysis was a precise one, and an accurate one. He concluded his speech by urging an extended and strengthened agitation, and a crofter offensive against the depradations of the landlords. It was a landmark speech. The viewpoint of the mass of the crofting people had at last been bluntly and publicly expressed; and the events in Kilmuir and in Leckmelm had attracted and focussed the attention of the latent pro-crofter movement; for the first time ever, indeed, there was a movement capable of action against the landlords.

Hearing of the dispute in Kilmuir, John Murdoch went to Skye, and in the Braes district close to Portree, sold a dozen subscriptions to *The Highlander* among Lord MacDonald's tenants there. In Glasgow, at an Irish anti-landlord meeting in support of Parnell, resolutions of support for the Skye crofters were moved; the following month, the Federation of Celtic Societies minuted its support; and the formation of a Skye Vigilance Committee was reported. And as a result of the Leckmelm protest meeting in Inverness, Fraser-Mackintosh was finally convinced by Mackenzie that it was high time to begin pressing the Government to appoint a Royal Commission to inquire into Highland affairs and the grievances of the crofting population. The Government, and the landed rich generally, would resist; but their resistance was quickly to be overtaken by events, beside which recent stirrings of protest and discontent were made to appear pale and insignificant.

The winter of 1881 was a severe one, and as the year drew to its end, great gales swept across the islands. In November, twelve hundred boats were damaged and destroyed, and a fund was established in Glasgow for the relief of the even greater distress now prevalent in the islands and on the west coast of the Highlands. And in Glendale, in the west of Skye, the following spring brought further trouble. The district had been deliberately overcrowded by the landlords in the 1840s, the people being driven there to make what living they could from their little patches of land, and from the sea; that spring, however, the people of Glendale at last resolved to resist oppression. The local landowners had of late become increasingly oppressive. The crofters had already been forbidden to keep dogs; and then, suddenly, they were forbidden to search for driftwood on the seashore. On the fourth day of the New Year, the estate management displayed, in the local post office, a notice stating that, whereas the local people had been in the habit of trespassing on the lands of Glendale, Lorgill, Ramasaig and Waterstein, while searching for and carrying away drift timber, 'notice is hereby given that the shepherds and herds on these lands have instructions to give up the names of any persons found hereafter on any part of the said lands, as also anyone found carrying away timber from the shore by boats or otherwise, that they may be dealt with according to law.'

Confined thus to their own patches of land and forbidden even to walk on the hills that surrounded them, the Glendale people met at their church on 7 February 1882 at one o'clock in the afternoon, 'for the purpose of stating our respective grievances publicly, in order to communicate the same to our superiors'. At the meeting, it was decided that each township should petition for redress of its grievances; and the spirit of determination and unity was such that it was agreed, in writing, that they would tolerate no victimisation of any kind. The tenants of Skinidin demanded the grazing of islands in Loch Dunvegan, just opposite their crofts. Those of Colbost demanded reductions in their rents. In Hamaraverin, they demanded restitution of lands taken from them by the factor thirteen years previously. The people of Milovaig and Borodal wanted land in Waterstein. In Holmisdal too, the call was for more land; and the tenants of Glasvein petitioned for grazing land and peat moss.

Thus did the crofters of Glendale petition their landlords. Just eighteen months later the Glendale factor, writing about recent events in the district, talked of 'notorious agitators', and of 'simple minded but imaginative men … induced by fomenters of discontent', as a preamble to declaring his conscientious conviction that 'emigration on a pretty extensive scale was the only effectual measure for improving the conditions of the people.' He regretted very much, he said, 'the unreasoning opposition which has been manifested to this proposal, an opposition which there cannot be a shadow of doubt has been originated and is kept alive by gentlemen who should know better'.

But by then the people of Glendale did 'know better', in a different sense of the words. In the time-honoured tradition of Highland landlordism, their petitions had been summarily rejected. In response, the crofters promptly declared a rent-strike and drove their hungry cattle on to the farm of Waterstein. The estate management turned to the ever-obliging courts of law, and secured from the Court of Session an order requiring the crofters to remove their stock from the private grass of Waterstein. The order was ignored, and the cattle stayed on Waterstein. Temporarily, at least, the landlords and the law were stopped in their tracks. An uneasy peace settled on Glendale, and on the island of Skye; it was a peace that was not to last longer than a matter of weeks.

The Battle of the Braes

'Highlanders have not yet come to appreciate the true dignity of ordinary labour ...'

THE DUKE OF ARGYLL

Peace had hardly fallen on Glendale when, in the spring of 1882, there was another violent incident on Skye, this time on the opposite side of the island, in the district of Braes. Braes lies by the seashore, some miles to the south of Portree, and facing east across the narrows of Raasay Sound. In the 1840s, the minister of the district had described how the kind of husbandry prevalent in his parish was performed with the crooked spade, an instrument he reckoned 'most awkward' in appearance and operation, but very suitable for the land worked by the crofters of Braes, which was 'for the most part hanging on steep braes and precipices, and encumbered with rocks and ponderous stones'.

By the 1880s conditions had, if anything, changed for the worse for the tenants of Braes. Their complaints were familiar ones in the Highlands: poor land, high rents and insufficient ground; while all around were great tracts under sheep and deer. The Braes townships, Balmeanach, Peinchorran, and Gedintailor, were owned by Lord MacDonald—a small part of his 140,000 acre estate—while just to the south of Braes, by Loch Sligachan, he owned a 10,000 acre deer-forest, running over fine grazing-land right down to the seashore.

Lord MacDonald was rather different from the usual run of landowner in the Highlands at that time. More typical were incomers or investors from the south—men like Messrs. Ramsden, Ellice and Chisholm-Batten, and the Duke of Richmond, who between them held 90,000 acres of

Armadale Castle, Skye. In the middle of the nineteenth century, Robert Somers wrote, 'The effect was the same as when a hawker of the backwoods spreads out his toys and trinkets and fire-waters before a tribe of Indians. The vanity of the Highland chiefs was intoxicated...There is a staircase-window in Lord MacDonald's mansion in Skye which is said to have cost £500'.

Inverness-shire for sporting purposes. Though the MacDonald family had once considered mining coal in the parish of Portree, their wealth and standing were derived not from the slums and factories of the industrial heartlands, but from the traditional MacDonald lands and tenantry. One of the most illustrious Highland families of old, they were well used to ruling over land and people. They were also a family of soldiers: MacDonald himself had served in the Highland Light Infantry; and in the coming years his sons would fight and die for the British Empire against the Boer and the German. But despite these differences of background, the effect was essentially the same: although MacDonald might enjoy certain residual loyalties that were denied to the new, southern breed of landlord, it was as a landlord that he held his estates, whether he dined in the splendour of Armadale Castle, dourly overlooking the Sound of Sleat and the barren hills of Knoydart and Morar and Moidart, or in the Carlton Club in London.

In the running of his domains Lord MacDonald was assisted by one of his own name, Alexander MacDonald, a solicitor in Portree and his Lordship's factor for the townships in Braes. This factor was a most powerful man in the administration of Skye. He was clerk of the peace for the island, a bank agent, a landowner in his own right, factor for five estates, secretary to or a member of every school board, a member of every parochial board, and a captain in the local militia. He was also a deputy sheriff-officer, a clerk to the road trustees, and a collector of the poor rates. But powerful though he and his lordly employer were, they were, that spring of 1882, to confront a greater power—that of the united crofting tenants of Braes.

The people of Braes saw their grievances increasingly championed in Parliament, in the House of Commons at least. They saw a popular victory in Glendale, and another in Kilmuir. They knew that the Federation of Celtic Societies in Glasgow had formed a Skye Vigilance Committee. John Murdoch had visited the district and *The Highlander* was circulating freely among the Braes crofters. Government agents were shortly to report that 'publications of socialist tendency were, and still are, circulated among the population through agencies in London and other large towns'. And in the previous summer, as these agents noted with alarm, men from Braes had been at the fishing off Ireland, sailing from the anti-landlord stronghold of Kinsale. The time had come to go on the offensive—and as an objective they chose the recovery of their former grazing-land on nearby Ben Lee, of which they had been summarily deprived in the 1860s. Accordingly, in November, 1881, the tenants of Braes petitioned for the restoration of their grazing rights on Ben Lee. The petition was despatched to Lord MacDonald, who summarily rejected it. At that, the tenants of Braes marched into the factor's office in Portree with the message that they intended to pay no further rent until such time as their demand for the grazing of Ben Lee was met; and having calmly delivered that ultimatum, the men of Braes went home again.

In the eyes of the propertied class, the people of Braes had committed a most heinous crime. Lord MacDonald demanded that his tenants be tried, convicted, and gaoled for criminal intimidation. It was not a charge that any Highland landlord had ever faced; but as it was now merely tenants who were concerned, the judicial authorities gave it their grave consideration. After much thought they decided against such a course—on the grounds that they might lose the contest for insufficient evidence. Rather, they counselled Lord MacDonald to attempt some intimidation himself—intimidation of a sort which, being within the law, would not be criminal. Lord MacDonald resolved on this course of lawful action—the traditional remedy for insubordination—and selected the names of a dozen or so tenants; his intention was to have them evicted, so that their fellows might come to their senses, desist from their sedition, and return peacefully to their allocated place in society. It was a reasonable strategy, which had served MacDonald and his kind perfectly well for generations.

But it was not to work in the townships of Braes. The exemplary evictions were to be effected in April, 1882; and in the first week of that month, Martin, the agent for the estate, left Portree to deliver the notices of eviction. Martin was the sheriff-officer of the district; he was also deputy to the estate factor, who in turn was deputy sheriff-officer. As Martin and his two assistants approached Braes, two boys on lookout for his approach gave warning of it, and a mile before they reached the townships, they were met by between a hundred and fifty and two hundred people. The eviction party was halted and surrounded; the summonses were taken from Martin and he was compelled to burn them; and he was then chased from Braes with the warning that should he return he would not live to tell the tale.

Deforcement such as this was a criminal offence; and the authorities saw it as an opportunity, in the words of another Skye landlord, to 'stamp out quickly the first germs of anything like the Irish disease'. Exemplary action in Braes, it was thought, would both destroy resistance there and discourage agitation elsewhere in the Highlands; and in particular, the Sheriff of Inverness-shire, William Ivory, saw it as an excellent opportunity to crush once and for all crofter resistance in the Isle of Skye. The authorities decided to arrest hostages from among the Braes tenantry and deal them a sentence of such severity as would stifle further agitation for good. However, the constables of Skye were of doubtful loyalty in such a confrontation as was now planned, and in any case could not have effected arrests in Braes, even if they had been prepared to try. And from the whole of Inverness-shire, only 19 constables could be made available for special service in Skye, a number which was adjudged quite insufficient for the hazardous duty now required of them. Ivory's deputy wanted 100 soldiers; but consultation at the highest Government level led the Lord Advocate to detail fifty police from the Glasgow force to proceed north. With them went a press corps the like of which had never been seen in the Highlands. From the *Glasgow Citizen* came Macleod Ramsay, who arrived on the same steamer as the force of police. There were representatives of the *Scotsman*, the *Glasgow Herald*, the *North British Daily Mail* and the *Inverness Courier* in Skye that week. The sub-editor of the *Northern Chronicle* came to the island, and the editor of the *Courier* came in person. The *Glasgow News* and the *Freeman's Journal* had men in Skye too, and others were on their way north; it was reported that the *London Standard* had despatched to Skye no less a man than its war correspondent.

The Highland crofters' cause was suddenly newsworthy. The national newspapers were, almost without exception, vehemently anti-crofter; it was said of the *Scotsman* that 'it hates the crofters a great deal more than Satan'. But whatever its bias, the national press was that week—for the first time ever—exhibiting a keen interest in and coverage of anti-landlord action in the Highlands; and the resultant publicity was in the end to benefit none more than the crofting population. Mr Ramsay's paper prefaced his reports with the editorial comment that it had been a matter of common report for some months past that, in the Isle of Skye and in the other more remote parts of the Highlands, 'doctrines have been disseminated regarding the rights of occupancy which were not calculated to promote' what the *Citizen* liked to regard as the real interests of the crofters. Mr Ramsay himself thought that sedition was rampant in Skye. At the beginning of the week, he telegrammed south from Oban; that morning at dawn the steamer carrying the police reinforcements had put in to the bay, with the police sealed below-decks and none allowed ashore. Lord MacDonald's castle was let out at the time, and he himself was sojourning in Nice—a fact which Ramsay could have mentioned when he described how the Braes tenants had at one time been loyal and 'even affectionate'; but now, and for the past two years, every recurring rent-payment had induced growing signs of rebelliousness. According to the *Citizen*, events in Skye bore witness to the 'lamentable progress' which had been made in the dissemination of 'dangerous and pernicious doctrines'. No words could be too strong to condemn the 'incendiary language' used by the 'knot of individuals' who had formed themselves into the Skye Vigilance Committee; for they were all men of education and should know better than to behave as they were reported to be behaving. The recent developments in Skye were much too serious to allow of such irresponsible misuse of knowledge. There were many thousands of crofters in Skye, reported Ramsay before sailing north from Oban, 'and it is feared that if the refusal to pay rents is not crushed-out, in its initial stages, it may spread ... throughout the island'.

It was not until one in the morning that the steamer finally reached Portree, and though the plan of Sheriff Ivory had been to land his men at once from the *Clansman*, and proceed in the dark towards Braes, her skipper grounded her just off the pier, and an hour or more was lost in refloating her. Another hour was lost too, once the party was finally ashore, when Angus Martin refused Ivory's instruction to accompany the expedition and assist in identifying ringleaders of the sedition. Thus, by the time that the party finally got under way, 'the grey dawn of the morning was suffusing the sky'. To make their discomfort greater it began to rain, the drizzle 'ere long increasing to driving showers of unusual severity'. The procession, thought Mr Gow of the *Dundee Advertiser*, wore a sombre aspect that was not helped by the 'sheer brutal ferocity' of the weather. All told, nearly sixty men marched south to Braes that morning—two sheriffs, two fiscals, near to fifty police from Glasgow, some local police, and the gentlemen of the press. Ivory rode towards the rear of the procession, in a carriage requisitioned for the occasion; but four miles from Braes he abandoned it, and joined his men on the waterlogged track winding south through the rain. At seven o'clock the party finally reached Braes. To their surprise no trouble was encountered, and Gedintailor township 'was passed without any demonstration of hostility'. Inspector Cameron, however, believed it quite certain that their return passage would be disputed; and his fears were to be amply justified. The party lost no time, and had no difficulty, in arresting its chosen hostages from the Braes townships; but its return with them to Portree was the cause of an encounter both more violent and more extensive than any yet witnessed in the growing agitation.

The arrests themselves were not disputed; but the attempt to remove the prisoners from Braes led to an immediate riot. The women, 'with the most violent gestures and imprecations' declared that the police must be attacked, and at once stones began to be thrown. The police drew their batons and charged. As Gow reported, this was the signal for a general attack. 'Huge boulders darkened the horizon as they sped from the hands of infuriated men and women. Large sticks and flails were brandished and brought down with crushing force upon the police ... Many were struck, and a number more or less injured.' To the man from the *Advertiser*, the situation was highly dangerous for the police: maddened by the apprehension of some of the oldest men in the township, the crofters rushed on the police, each armed with heavy stones, 'which, on approaching near enough, they discharged with a vigour that nothing could resist'. The women of Braes, thought Gow, were if anything even more determined and aggressive than the men; and though the police baton-charged twice, they still approached to within a few yards, 'and poured a fearful volley into the compact mass of the police. The situation was indeed serious; a throng of crofters now barred the route of the party back to Portree, and Gow observed hundreds of determined-looking persons converging on the procession; a rush had to be made, or there was the likelihood of Ivory himself being assaulted. Ramsay saw the sheriff fall at least twice in the riot; and though at that moment the police smashed their way through the barrier of crofters, it was with some difficulty and much anger that Ivory returned to Portree. After that final serious scrimmage, said Gow, no further demonstration of hostility was offered, 'and the procession went on, without further adventure, to Portree ... All arrived at their destination completely exhausted. On arrival in the town the police were loudly hooted and hissed as they passed through the square to the gaol, and subsequently when they marched from the Court House to the Royal Hotel'.

David Gow's report from Skye remains to the present day one of the best-remembered accounts of the Battle of the Braes, as it was instantly named. Many others were sent south that week, and their effect was considerable. In the story of the Highland land agitation, the Battle of the Braes was the signal for an unprecedented level of agitation all over the Highlands; to the landowners and to the Government it seemed to rock the boat of Victorian Britain in a way reminiscent of the Highland insurrections of previous centuries; and for the emergent pro-crofter movement it was a test of will-power and solidarity. On the very day of the crofters' arrest arrangements for their defence were made in Inverness. In Glasgow, too, a defence committee sprang into existence. The prisoners were held until the end of April, when they were charged with assault and deforcement, and committed for trial in Inverness. Bail, fixed at £20 each, was subscribed by eight citizens of that town and the crofters returned home, by train to Strome Ferry, and thence by steamer to Portree, where a tumultuous welcome awaited them. The authorities attempted to deny the crofters' cause the publicity attendant on a jury trial, and insisted that the Braes men be tried summarily before a sheriff. The defence lawyers objected, writing to the Lord Advocate that, 'the object of your order is to secure their conviction at all hazards irrespective of their guilt or innocence'. Questions were asked in the House of Commons; and Fraser-Mackintosh wrote to the *Times* to protest, asking why, if the Lord Advocate insisted on a summary trial, it was to be conducted in Inverness, when summary cases relating to Skye were always tried in Portree?

The authorities, however, would not change their minds; and at noon on 11th May, the men of Braes appeared at the bar of the Sheriff Court in Inverness Castle, charged with 'deforcing an officer of the law in the execution of his duty; or of the crime of violently resisting and obstructing an officer of the law in the execution of his duty, or persons employed by and assisting an officer of the law in the execution of his duty; and also of the crime of assault'. They denied the charges, and evidence was led. They were found guilty, and fined, with the alternative of imprisonment. Supporters in court at once paid the fines; the Federation of Celtic Societies paid the other costs. The crofters returned to Skye; and the tenants of Braes drove their stock to Ben Lee to enjoy there Lord MacDonald's good grazing. MacDonald's Edinburgh agents demanded by registered post that they desist, but the people refused to accept the letters. The Court of Session issued writs against the Braes crofters, but the officers carrying them were driven away. The cattle stayed on Ben Lee, and no one could do anything about it.

Skye was now officially considered to be in a state of lawlessness, and what was feared most in government circles was that the disease might prove to be infectious. By late summer, the authorities feared that a rent-strike would soon be in operation across the whole island; a month later they feared that the whole Highland people would be on strike, seizing their forefather's land, defying Government authority, and challenging the very order of society. Sheriff Ivory was demanding that a warship and marines be ordered north to quell Skye; so nervous were the authorities that the Lord Advocate agreed; and they all agreed that there must not be another Braes incident.

For Braes had been a remarkable victory; its effect on crofter morale across the Highlands was immense; and its example and lessons were swiftly and eagerly emulated. In the district of Lochcarron at the time of the Braes dispute, eviction orders were served on two local crofters, by name of Mackenzie and Maclean. Maclean was eighty-one years old and bedridden, and his wife was over seventy; he had worked his croft for sixty years. Mackenzie was in his sixties and had been a crofter for over forty years. In the spring of 1882, however, their landlord resolved to turn them out of their homes—as a punishment for the doings of others. In the previous March their sons, George Mackenzie and Donald Maclean, who were masons living on their fathers' crofts, had contracted with the estate factor to construct a sheep-pen for him. The work was done, and a dispute over payment ensued. When the two sons remonstrated, the landlords's agent defamed them; and they won an action for damages in the Sheriff Court. Since they did not occupy crofts of their own, the landlord determined to avenge their temerity in taking his agent to court, by the expedient of evicting the parents. A sheriff-officer and party were summoned from Dingwall, duly arrived in Lochcarron, and started to empty the Mackenzie home of the family's hard-won belongings and effects. A crowd of crofters gathered from miles around; and though police were summoned, the sheriff-officer was deforced, and the Mackenzies' belongings were reinstated by the crowd. The authorities did not dare, on this occasion, to prosecute for criminal deforcement: the procurator-fiscal, who would have been responsible for such a prosecution, had himself been the landlord's agent for the attempted eviction; and the publicity from Braes, and the authorities' fear of inciting a generalised anti-landlord agitation in Ross-shire, dissuaded them from immediate action.

The landlord retreated, and sold the estate; and the authorities switched their attentions back to Skye, and the seditious state of the crofting population in Glendale. Throughout 1882, the people of Glendale maintained their rent-strike and kept their stock on the forbidden grazing-land. The estate had appealed, as other estates had so often done in the past, to the Court of Session, which granted an order instructing the crofters to remove their stock. But this order simply could not be enforced, or even served; for although Glendale was officially in need of policing, no policeman or law-officer dared enter it. In January, 1883, a force of police was sent into Glendale to re-establish the rule of law in the west of Skye. The people were ready for them, and around five hundred men armed with sticks set upon them and drove them from the estate back towards Dunvegan. And some days afterwards, armed with sticks and graips and scythes, hundreds of men marched on Dunvegan to drive the police from the entire district; the police took to the hills, and fled before them. At this point the authorities were forced to take really determined steps to crush resistance in Glendale, and they determined at first to send in a gunboat and marines. At the last minute, however, it was decided instead to send with the gunboat, instead of marines, a Government representative to demand that the people surrender hostages. After discussion, this demand was accepted, and the hostages were gaoled for two months in the Calton Gaol in Edinburgh. It was reported that in the evenings supporters in the town arranged for the playing of bagpipes in the vicinity of the gaol, so that the prisoners might be enlivened and encouraged by the music of the instrument which had always accompanied Highlanders into battle. On 15 May, the Glendale hostages were freed, and set out to return home to Skye; since their imprisonment, there had been great developments in the crofters' cause.

Her Majesty's Commission

*'When I came to the country the
clearances in 1851, and the emigration,
forced in some cases with circumstances
of shocking brutality, were fresh in the
memory of old and young ...
In the evidence given by the crofters'
delegates ... there was nothing ...
that I did not hear long ago in every
part of the parish, from the Sound of
Barra to the North Ford. To say,
as has been said, that they only
repeated the lessons taught them by
agitators, means saying that they learned
the lesson long years before agitators
or a Royal Commission ... were dreamt of.
They did not exaggerate. Indeed, in
describing things that happened in those
times, to exaggerate would not be easy.'*

DONALD MACKINTOSH

The winter of 1882-1883 was a bad one in the Highlands, the weather severe and food scarce. The very poor potato crop meant that by the spring of 1883, a third of the families in Kilmuir were destitute. In Argyll, conditions were even worse; and everywhere, the people were compelled to throw themselves on the mercy of the savagely-managed Destitution Fund. The autumn herring-fishing had gone badly, with the shoals absent from the lochs and the coast; and in October, gales and rain had ruined the grain standing in the fields; across the Highlands, crofters faced slow starvation. Many ministers were counselling submission to this act of inscrutable, but benign, Providence; but the crofting community had developed rather different ideas about the sources of its poverty and hunger.

The events in Braes and Glendale and Lochcarron had been widely reported, and made a deep impression across the Highlands. Over the year, resistance to the landlords had flourished spectacularly. In Braes and Glendale, the people were defiant; and their example was copied more and more widely. The police, landlords' agents and sheriff-officers were denied effective access to more and more areas of the Highlands; and when they did enter them, they were attacked, deforced and driven from the district. In defiance of the law and its agents, lands were seized for the use and benefit of the people, and rent-strikes became even more widespread. In previously passive areas, especially in the islands, the crofters were giving every indication that they were about to repossess all the land that had been taken from them and their fathers, in the Clearances and since.

For the Government and the propertied rich, this was an alarming prospect: these events in the Highlands challenged the very basis of the Victorian social order; and there was the further fear that the defiant spirit of the crofters might spread, and infect the labouring millions in the cities. At first, the authorities favoured the traditional response of sending in the military, of despatching gunboats and marines to settle the Highland land question. At the end of 1882, the Lord Advocate had convinced Harcourt, the Home Secretary, of the need for force. Harcourt believed that any lesser action might be taken to imply that the Government thought the crofters did have legitimate grievances; but he was particularly anxious to avoid the danger of 'opening the flood-gates of a Highland land question'. In September of that year, the Lord Advocate had reckoned that a formal inquiry, such as the crofters were everywhere demanding, would be the signal for increased and extended agitation; for it would give rise to 'an unsettled feeling among the smaller tenantry, and would lead to their cherishing hopes which would ultimately be disappointed'. The Highland landlords, fearful of what an official investigation might reveal, were equally opposed to any such notion; it could lead, in the words of the Duke of Argyll, to a further 'unsettlement on all ideas of property'.

At the same time, some Government action was imperative, given that Highland estates were actually being taken over by the crofters. Military intervention was acceptable so long as it was certain of having the desired effect; but by the end of 1882 this could no longer be guaranteed, unless by a full-scale military invasion, which, for obvious reasons, the Government could not countenance. Moreover, there were doubts as to the loyalty of the Highland recruits on which the British army as a whole relied heavily. Again, military intervention would be a dangerous stimulant to the already high morale of the people. By the end of the year, Harcourt was convinced that the demand to send troops to Skye to collect Lord MacDonald's rents was 'a very serious business', which, if carried out, would lead to very grave consequences. The use of troops in this kind of agrarian dispute was 'in the highest degree impolitic, and with a dour folk like the Scotch most dangerous. It will bring up the land question in the Highlands in a form which the lairds will bitterly regret.'

The Government and landlords, though greatly alarmed, saw no obvious remedy for the spreading agitation; and while they hesitated the crofters' movement continued to grow. For long enough, spokesmen for the crofters' cause had been urging the Government to appoint a Royal Commission. As long ago as October, 1877, Alexander Mackenzie of the *Celtic Magazine* had asked Fraser-Mackintosh whether he would press in Parliament for the formation of a Commission 'to inquire into the present impoverished and wretched conditions and, in some places, the scarcity of men and women in the Highlands; and the most effectual remedy for ameliorating the condition of the Highland crofters generally'. At that time Fraser-Mackintosh had thought that it would be counter-productive to press for a Commission, unless the request was strengthened by a general expression of feeling in its favour throughout the country. The years following 1877 did indeed witness an increase in the expression of crofters' feelings on their conditions; and soon the Gaelic Society of Inverness was petitioning for a Royal Commission. In late 1880, at the Leckmelm protest meeting at which the Reverend MacMillan spoke so ably, Fraser-Mackintosh agreed that the time was now ripe to raise the matter in Parliament. When the Edinburgh Sutherland Association met in January 1882, Professor Blackie argued from the platform that the principle of the Irish Land Act applied to the Highlands as well as to Ireland, and that principle was that the people had a right to the soil. 'This was their favourable moment,' Blackie counselled: 'this was the moment when they must speak out.'

In September of that year, a deputation of crofters' spokesmen and supporters visited Fraser-Mackintosh in the Royal Hotel in Inverness, to impress upon him the necessity of energetic action in Parliament, to obtain a special inquiry, by a Royal Commission, into the crofter question. The matter was pressed hard by the Federation of Celtic Societies, and by the Gaelic Society of Perth; and across the country well-attended meetings reinforced the demand. In February, 1883, in Edinburgh, 2,500 people packed out a meeting which unanimously carried three motions demanding the appointment of a Royal Commission. The Reverend Begg, seconded by Donald MacFarlane, Member of Parliament for County

Carlow, proposed the motion that the meeting viewed with alarm the prevailing condition of the Highlands, and called upon the Government to appoint a Royal Commission to examine the alleged grievances of the people there, and the extensive depopulation of fertile districts for purposes of sport. Professor Blackie called on the meeting to recognise the need for united action on the part of all friends of the Highlands, and went on to demand legal security for the Highland crofter against capricious eviction and rack-renting; the amelioration of their conditions generally; the collection of information regarding the extensive occupation of the Highlands by deer-forests; an agitation for their destruction; and an end to further depopulation of productive districts for such purposes. Blackie concluded with an appeal for combined action in favour of the changes in the land laws necessary to secure the objects he had proposed. Even the Free Church was now demanding reforms in the crofters' favour, inasmuch as the prominent figure of Robert Rainy addressed that same meeting to ask for restraint in the abuse of landlord power.

Institutional support for the crofters' cause had now spread far beyond the Gaelic and Highland and Celtic Societies of the southern towns. The voice of the Free Church, with its mass following in the Highlands, and considerable authority among crofters, was a most important addition to the cause, though its support was, of course, limited by doctrinal considerations. As Rainy himself commented later on, it was well remembered in Sutherland how, 'at the time of the changes there, wild talk and wild plans among the younger men were repressed by the resolute determination of the leading religious people to have nothing to do with any plans that proposed to avert sufferings by sinning'. To him, and to others like him, the Free Church could have no sort of sympathy with any who made it their object to lead the people to resistance of the law, or into collision with the law; the land question must be solved, 'not with the desire of dividing class from class, or sacrificing the interests of any class'.

The growing agitation, both in the House of Commons and in the country at large, began to convince the Government that it would be wiser to accede to popular demand. In November 1882, when Donald MacFarlane asked the Prime Minister whether the steps the Government was proposing to take with regard to the Highland crofters included the establishment of a Royal Commission, Gladstone replied that no such question was under the consideration of Her Majesty's Government. But by then even the Home Secretary, whose knowledge of the Highlands was confined to police reports and stalking holidays there, was beginning to realise that a tactical retreat was the best response to the agitation. Over the winter, Fraser-Mackintosh, MacFarlane and Charles Cameron pressed the matter; in February, twenty-one Scottish Members of Parliament wrote to Harcourt asking for a Commission; and on the 23rd of the same month Fraser-Mackintosh himself wrote to Harcourt.

He had never before taken up the Home Secretary's time, he wrote, either by letter or interview, with reference to the state of the crofter and

'Events now occurring render inquiry imperative...it will be imprudent to delay'. Charles Fraser-Mackintosh, Royal Commissioner and Crofters' Member for Inverness-shire.

rural population of the Highlands and Islands of Scotland; but now he felt constrained to do so. It was upwards of two years since he had presided at a public meeting in Inverness, where the subject was discussed, and an inquiry demanded. He had attempted to raise the question in the House of Commons in the summer of 1881, he reminded Harcourt, and again early in 1882. He had tabled a motion urging the appointment of a Royal Commission, for he felt very unhappy at the present state of affairs, and believed that many of his countrymen were looking to him for parliamentary assistance; and he begged to remind Harcourt that the mass of the people in the Highlands were in favour of an inquiry. He also reminded the Home Secretary of the petition from Glendale presented by him the previous Wednesday, which represented the 'true and un-prompted' feelings of the crofters there, and likewise asked for an official inquiry. 'The public in Scotland by numerous meetings and otherwise show that they concur ... The press of Scotland, from the *Scotsman* downwards, may be said to be unanimous'. Neither was there any opposition from the landlords generally, and the officials in the disturbed districts were not averse to the idea; and lastly, he had felt it his duty, within the previous two or three days, to test the opinion of the Scottish Members of the House on the matter. Seven of their number were in the Government; one was sick; that left fifty-two. Of those, several were not in London, but two of them were known to have expressed themselves publicly in favour of an inquiry. And of those to whom he had appealed, twenty-one had not been opposed to an inquiry. Seven, though they would have hesitated to agree in public, had also expressed their approval. He had only found four decidedly hostile to the idea; and he therefore felt able 'to assure you that a large majority of the unofficial Scottish members are favourable'. This fact, coupled with what had already been shown to be the case, should prompt the Government to delay no longer. For his own part, he could not have believed that so soon after the meeting at Inverness in December 1880, the agitation should have gone to such a pitch. And though he was 'as clear as anyone that the law should be upheld, yet it will be imprudent to delay'.

With the exception of Fraser-Mackintosh himself, not one single member from the Highlands would add his signature to the petition for an inquiry, which the Member for Inverness enclosed with his letter; the other twenty-one Members of Parliament who had signed it all represented southern Scottish constituencies. By now, however, the Highland Members' opposition to inquiry mattered little: the demands for a Commission had become irresistible. On the very eve of the announcement of the Commission, Mackenzie's *Celtic Magazine* kept up the pressure, interpreting the failure of any Highland member except Fraser-Mackintosh to support the demand for an inquiry as Highland landlord opposition to a Commission. Mackenzie himself wrote that this alone should convince the Government of the necessity of making the Royal Commission really effective, by placing upon it men who would counteract the landlord opposition and aristocratic influence, which would certainly have to be met in the course of the inquiry, on every point where the facts were likely to tell against the landlords and their agents. 'Unless the other side is strongly represented, so as to meet, on something like equal ground, the power, wealth and influence of those whose conduct has made this inquiry necessary,' wrote Mackenzie, 'the Royal Commission had better never to have been granted. It will only prove the commencement of an agitation, on the land question, the end of which no one can predict ... If it fails to give satisfaction, the people, by a more powerful, legitimate, and persistent action, will still have the remedy in their own hands.'

Towards the end of February, the mounting flood of demands, and the dangerous situation in Skye, forced the Government to move. On the 26th of that month the appointment of a Royal Commission was announced. Governmental resistance to inquiry had dissolved in the face of concerted public demand—and also, doubtless, from a realisation that this course of action need not be wholly detrimental to the landed cause. For one thing, it would terminate divisive debate as to whether recalcitrant tenantry should be dealt with by repression or by appeasement. It might serve to postpone the day of radical change; and anticipation of its results would, hopefully, still the voice of agitation. Again, if the Commissioners were suitably chosen, no conclusion or proposal would emerge contrary to the landlord interest.

On 17 March, 1883, the Royal Warrant was given to appoint Her Majesty's 'trusty and well-beloved' Commissioners, 'to inquire into the conditions of the Crofters and Cottars in the Highlands and Islands of Scotland, and all matter affecting the same, or relating thereto'. There were six Commissioners; four landed proprietors, one lawyer who was also the son of a landowner, and the newly-appointed Professor of Celtic at Edinburgh University—a Highlander from Colonsay by birth, but by training a philosopher and scholar with no sympathy for the politics of land reform. Fraser-Mackintosh himself was a member; his was a shrewd appointment, calculated to induce among crofters a belief that the Commission was bi-partisan at least, if not unbiased. The same might be said about Mackinnon, in view of the pride many Highlanders felt about the establishment of the Celtic Chair. The composition of the remainder, however, indicated only too well that whatever it might recommend, the Royal Commission would not operate, in Principal Rainy's words, 'with the desire of dividing class from class, or sacrificing the interests of any class'. The Chairman of the Commission was Francis Napier, Baron of Napier and Ettrick. Educated at Trinity College, Cambridge, he was an Anglican Tory, a landowner, and a career diplomat with considerable former experience of colonial problems and administration in India; his home address was a castle in Selkirk.

Commissioner Alexander Nicolson, although of Skye extraction, was the Sheriff-substitute of Kirkcudbright and an advocate at the Edinburgh Bar, and had thus a very great deal in common with the sheriffs, advocates,

Lord Napier, chairman of the Royal Commission. He wrote, 'In the Highlands and Islands
...the two factors in the quarrel stand face to face; on the one side is the vacant land, on the
other side the craving multitude'.

and judges who had for generations defended the landlord interest in the Highlands. The fifth member of the Commission was Sir Kenneth Mackenzie of Gairloch, the owner of close on 170,000 acres in the Highlands, 43,000 acres of them in one deer-forest alone. His education had taken the form of private tuition; he was Lord Lieutenant of Ross and Cromarty, and convener of its County Council. Cameron of Lochiel, the sixth Commissioner, had much in common with Mackenzie. Married to the daughter of a Duke, this latter-day Highland chieftain had been educated at Harrow. He too was Lord Lieutenant of his county, Inverness, and convener of its County Council; he was also a Member of Parliament and the owner of a deer-forest of 8,000 acres.

These men, with the exception of Fraser-Mackintosh, included no-one who was qualified by personal experience and sympathy to consider the problems and aspirations of the Highland crofting community. The Commission, in short, was heavily weighted in favour of the propertied élite, and could hardly be expected to issue proposals of the kind that would benefit the Highland crofter; for such proposals would inevitably and fundamentally damage the landed interest. The composition of the Commission was at once denounced by the crofters' spokesmen as one-sided and antagonistic to the interests of the Highland people. In the *Celtic Magazine*, Alexander Mackenzie fulminated vehemently against its membership. 'How have the government acted? They have appointed a Commission that has been universally condemned by every association, every individual ... In that condemnation ... we are compelled to join'. Nothing would satisfy the public, he continued, short of making the cruel evictions of the past impossible in future in the Highlands, by giving the people a permanent interest in the soil they cultivated. 'That a recommendation to that effect can emanate from a Royal Commission composed as this one is, is scarcely conceivable ... Are Sir Kenneth Mackenzie and Lochiel, for instance, at all likely to recommend the modification of their present rights of property, or the abolition or material curtailment of deer-forests, from which they and their class derive a great portion of their revenues? If they do so they will prove themselves more than human.'

The landlords, for their part, were delighted with the composition of the Commission. The *Scotsman*, the *Northern Chronicle*, and the *Inverness Courier*, 'three newspapers whose position in the past has been one of strong and long-sustained antagonism and misrepresentation of the Highland peasantry, and, at the same time, of powerful and steady support of their oppressors', approved thoroughly of the Government's choice of members. And such was the landlord's faith in the Commissioners that the Skye factor, Donald MacDonald of Tormore, predicted that the result of the Commission would be to 'vindicate many sorely-maligned proprietors and factors from the charges made against them by untruthful outside agitators'.

The landlords were not disappointed. The Commission began its investigations on May 5th; it was to tour the Highlands for five months, concluding the 'active part of our mission' on October 24th. In those five months, the Commissioners held seventy-one meetings, in sixty-one places, and took evidence from almost eight hundred people—crofters, landlords, factors, and ministers. They left from Oban, aboard the *Lively*, and sailed north for Skye, through the Sounds of Mull and Sleat and Raasay, and arrived at Portree, from whence they journeyed south to Braes. Their first public meeting was held there on May 8th. In Braes, and throughout Skye, much of the crofters' testimony was given in Gaelic, as was that of the Commission's very first witness, Angus Stewart of Peinchorran. He asked for assurances that he would not be evicted for what he might tell the Commissioners. His landlord's agent refused to give such assurances; and Lord Napier too assured him that the Commission had no power to give him absolute security of the kind which he desired—'The Commission cannot interfere between you and your landlord, or between you and the law'. It was an inauspicious start to the work of the Commission; and Napier was to give many such disclaimers in the course of the next five months.

That day in Braes, they heard the evidence of eight crofters, one cottar, the factor, and the minister; even if they had proceeded no further, however, the evidence of their very first witness presented all the grievances that the Highland crofters would express over the coming five months. Angus Stewart told the Commission that the principal things he had to complain of was his poverty; and the way in which the poor crofters were huddled together, while the best part of the land was devoted to deer-forests and big farms. If they had plenty of land there would be no poverty in the Highlands. They were willing and able to work it. What would remedy the people's grievances throughout the Isle of Skye would be a sufficiency of land, as there was plenty of it, and they were willing to work it. He had to complain also of the rent that was charged them, and of their being deliberately overcrowded. He remembered the factor 'clearing a township and devoting the township's land to the purposes of the deer-forest—clearing them out of their houses and settling them down among the Braes'. The factor had settled a widow and her family down on his father's croft, with the intention that his father would share the peats and half of the croft with her; when he went to the factor to complain of this arrangement, the factor told him that, if he would not accept it, 'he would not have a sod on Lord MacDonald's property by the term'. It was a great hardship that all their earnings at the fishing, 'we have to put into meal for the support of our families, and that altogether because we have not land which will yield a crop, but land which has been cropped continuously for the past thirty years, within my own memory—continually cropping the same land'.

When Napier asked Stewart what remedies he would propose, Stewart replied without hesitation, 'Give us land out of the plenty of land that is about for cultivation ... That is the principal remedy that I see. Give us land at a suitable rent ... The suitable land surrounds us on every hand ... The whole of that land is suitable land for cultivation ... Unless we can get that, poverty will not be got out of the Isle of Skye.' Sheriff Nicolson asked Stewart about the croft land; it was rocky, mossy land, came the reply—so boggy that he might catch a deer on it; and other parts of it were as hard as adamant. In his grandfather's time there had been five tenants in his township, but now there were twenty-six or twenty-seven—some of them cleared to make way for the adjacent deer-forest. Sheriff Nicolson asked who had built the houses when the land was sub-divided; Stewart told him that it had been the crofters themselves. Nicolson asked whether they had had any assistance in the building; Stewart replied, 'May the Lord look upon you! I have seen myself compelled to go to the deer-forest to steal thatch—to steal the wherewith to thatch our houses. If we had not done so we should have had none.' Sir Kenneth asked whether the ruinous continuous cropping of the land was due to the shortage of land. Stewart answered that it was, and added that if the crofters left any land out of cultivation for any time at all, then they would simply starve. Sir Kenneth asked, 'Don't you think if you left part of it out, and introduced a better system of cultivation, you would get more crop from the half of it than you do now from the whole?' Angus Stewart's reply was bitter and telling. 'What would we cultivate,' he asked, 'if we were to leave half of it out? What would feed the cattle for us if we were to leave half of it out of cultivation?'

That exchange effectively concluded the Commissioners' examination of Angus Stewart. They were to examine more crofters that day in Braes, and many more that summer in the Highlands; but Stewart's testimony was in itself a devastating and conclusive indictment of property relations in the Highlands. It spoke of clearance and eviction and poverty, of despotism and intimidation and exploitation untrammelled by any notion of social justice. With devastating clarity it exposed the speciousness of every aspect of what the landlords and their agents liked to call 'agricultural improvement'. Stewart's evidence to the Commission also gave the lie to the overworked fiction of the press and the landlords' apologists, that the Highland crofters were natural paupers, inclined by choice to live in overcrowded squalor, by nature lazy and unwilling to attempt to improve their crofts. He had shown that no one living permanently at the very brink of starvation could be lazy, having constantly to reap the land and the sea and the sea-shore merely to sustain life. He had shown how the poverty of crofters was due, not to some metaphysical or economic 'necessity', but—very concretely—to rack-renting and the deliberate diminution of holdings. He had revealed the truth behind the fictions of Highland 'over-population' and the 'need' for emigration, showing how that over-population was, in fact, the result of a deliberate policy of overcrowding on the margins of the land—a practice which simultaneously provided the landlords with sheep-farms and deer-forests, and gave them the basis on which to squeeze the people out altogether when it suited them—on grounds of overcrowding and poverty! He had shown that the absence of a buoyant crofting economy was due not to crofters and crofting *per se*, but to the impossibility of the crofters saving enough to invest in a worthwhile way; it arose from the rack-renting which took away every penny of any surplus he might produce, and from the absence of any security of tenure, and from the absence of any compensation for improvement. Even if a crofter managed to improve his croft—which was made deliberately difficult by the landlords—he could still be ejected without any compensation whatsoever; and if he was allowed to remain, he would pay an increased rent corresponding to the enhanced value of his croft. Angus Stewart had shown too how the Highland crofters were forced to resort to a most inefficient form of cropping, which in time impoverished them even further, leaving them in circumstances such that any attempt to improve their lot would cause their precarious economy to collapse. His exposition was, to say the least, more cogent than the theorising evasions of men like the Rev. Fell of Carlisle, the Laird of Lismore, who was the author of the often-quoted statement that the crofters' lot was 'one of idleness, and, of necessity, penury'.

That summer, as the Commission toured the Highlands, it was to hear much more of the same kind of testimony. Until the middle of June, it cruised among the islands, when the *Lively* struck Chicken Rock off Lewis, and sank under it. The *North Star* replaced her, and in July the Commission sailed north to the Shetlands: 'Orkney, the northern and western shores of Sutherland, the western seaboard of Ross-shire, Inverness-shire, and Argyllshire, with its island dependencies, were then successively visited, and the engagement of the *North Star* having expired on the 11th of August, we again broke off work at Lismore on the 13th.' On October 4th they re-assembled at Lybster in Caithness, from which they 'passed to the interior and southern parts of Sutherland, from thence to the district of Easter Ross, and eventually to Inverness, the valley of the Spey, Glasgow and Edinburgh, concluding the active part of our mission on the 24th of October'.

Throughout their travels the Commissioners had heard from the crofters of the Highlands testimony substantially similar to that given by their first witness in Braes. In Arisaig the evidence given before them concerned an estate which typified in many ways the changing pattern of land-ownership in the nineteenth century Highlands. By 1883 that district was entirely in the hands of the Astley-Nicholson family. In the early 1830s the Clanranald family, bankrupt, had sold the Arisaig estate to Lady Ashburton; she kept it for four or five years, and then sold out to Lord Cranstoun, who kept it for another few years. Having failed in an attempt to clear the native population from the estate, Cranstoun in turn sold it to a Mr Mackay, who in 1851 sold it to F D P Astley. Astley's son held the estate for a few years, died, and was succeeded by his sister, Miss Astley, who in due course married a Nicholson, from which union the estate took its name. The other estate in the Arisaig district was the South Morar estate; bankrupted and in a 'state of nature', it had been administered for nearly fifty years by two congenital morons—*an dà amadan* ('the two fools') as they were known locally. In mid-century, it went to a Macdonell, and in 1878 the Astleys acquired it. When the Commission came to Arisaig, the crofters' spokesman was, as frequently, the minister. The Rev. Donald MacCallum was examined at length; his analysis only reinforced what the Commissioners had heard in the previous three months. His description of the history of Arisaig bore out, to a large extent, 'the general complaint of a very injudicious and unnecessary limitation' of the area and quality of the land at the disposal of the crofters. There was excellent arable land in the hands of three sheep-farmers; there was plenty of hill pasture, shared between their stock and the deer of the deer-forest; and the great mass of the population was confined to mere patches of the poorest land. 'Rents are complained of as being excessive,' he told the Commission, 'and as having been increased in many cases, not by agreement, but by the one-sided order of the proprietor.'

MacCallum described how the povery and overcrowding in the village of Arisaig had resulted directly from the clearing of good lands now in the hands of the sheep-farmers and sportsmen. These villagers had no crofts and were dependent on the most casual employment. MacCallum then cited the case of a local woman who had died of starvation the previous February, at a time when the estate manager was owing ten shillings to her son; this case had never undergone public investigation; but 'if instead of a human being dying of starvation, it had been the killing of a deer or the spearing of a salmon … it would not have been allowed to lie over'. MacCallum told too of the recently-introduced estate regulations, locally called the Seventeen Commandments. He spoke of the way in which the Astleys forced the people to overcrowd and then used this overcrowding as an excuse to push them out; of how sons were not allowed to stay on their parents' crofts after the age of twenty-one, but would not be given any other house or land in the district either; of how, under a new regulation, the crofters would henceforth need the landlord's permission even to dig a drain; of how a crofter was not allowed to improve his house; and of how the Astleys had evicted a hundred people from one small part of the estate alone. He concluded with the comment that, 'one does not like to say that these English and other folk have a positive hatred to the native Highlander; but there is something at the bottom of it'.

Other witnesses that day told how the Arisaig district had once been populous; how Clanranald could once raise four or five hundred men there; and how there was now nothing to be seen between Arisaig and Moidart but the ruins of houses. Colin MacDonald of Bunacaimb told how shiploads of people had been sent away from the district. MacCallum himself told the Commissioners how, thirty years before, 120 families had been sent to the Americas and elsewhere. Eneas Macdonell told Lord Napier that 'in Lord Cranstoun's time the first Clearances commenced in this country, and I was then a young boy almost; but I shall never forget the

'Why should we emigrate? There is plenty of waste land around us; for what is an extensive deer forest in the heart of the most fertile part of our land but waste land?'—Donald Macdonald, Back of Keppoch.

feelings of awe and fear that came over the people'.

But the most eloquent witness of the day was Donald MacDonald from Back of Keppoch, who not only knew the iniquities of the past, but also saw precisely what was required for the Highlands from the Government. What he wished to see, he told Lord Napier, was a means whereby the people could purchase the land they occupied at its real value; all the land which had been taken from them should be restored, and they should be free from fear of removal so long as they rendered a fair rent. Seeing that their forefathers had been there from time immemorial, he believed that they had as much right to live in comfort there as the proprietor. 'And as to emigration,' he added, 'what land has a greater right to sustain us than the land for which our forefathers suffered and bled? Why should we emigrate? There is plenty of waste land around us; for what is an extensive deer-forest but waste land? And there is far too much of that here. The deer-forest

64

itself, once land flowing with milk and honey, which supported scores of families, in comfort, but who, alas! are now, on account of the mania for sport, scattered over the wide world, is far better than all the land now cultivated by the poor crofters.' MacDonald's landlords did not contradict him: they chose to remain in their mansion, set in its beautiful woodlands and overlooking the loch from whose shores the Young Pretender had fled to foreign exile, and did not emerge to face the Commission. Certainly, they sent their factor, the solicitor Banks, to assure the Commissioners of their piety and benevolence; but their own reticence was surely a most damning contradiction of the claims of their hireling.

The following Saturday, the *North Star* took the Commissioners south, round the bleak promontory of Ardnamurchan and down the Sound of Mull, to Lochaline. There, in the village church, they heard the evidence of landlord 'improvement' in Morvern. In the half-century before their arrival, the population had fallen from over two thousand people to around eight hundred; and those who had not been cleared right out of the country had been removed from the land they had occupied for generations and driven down to the sea shore, where they would be less likely to get in the way of the sheep and the deer. Charles Cameron, a crofter from Acharacle, explained to Lord Napier how his daughter in England sent money to him regularly, to enable him to pay the rent his landlord demanded. He told how, on the south side of Ardnamurchan, where the land was good, the people had been removed down to narrow and small places by the shore, where some of them had still a cow's grass, and some of them had no land at all. Dugald M'Gregor of Ardtornish, a labourer almost seventy years of age, told the Commission how he had been evicted from his croft, forty years before, by Patrick Sellar; he added that the people thought it a great hardship that they could not get any land to cultivate, although an abundance of good land, formerly under cultivation, was going waste at their very doors. As in Arisaig, landlord policy in Morvern had deprived the crofters of a proper supply of milk; M'Gregor complained that the people felt very much the want of milk for their families. He knew that the want of good milk, such as most of them had been accustomed to in their younger days, had a deteriorating influence, especially upon their children. 'We are aware that a certain medical gentleman in another part, while being examined before the Commission, recommended cheap beer as a substitute for milk. The use and introduction of such a substitute for milk in rearing our offspring we, and we are sure all Highlanders, will repudiate with scorn. We look upon such a suggestion as an insult to us; and we cannot perceive why we should be deprived of the means of having a supply of good milk, so that the proprietor may obtain a few pounds more rent.'

The following Monday, on the island of Lismore, when Lord Napier suggested that there must be plenty of milk available there, Hugh Cameron of Killean replied that all the milk produced by the farmer's cattle on the island went to fatten his calves. In fact, the evidence the Royal Commission

'Of what they had before the late conquest of their country, there remains only their language and their poverty'—a crofter's family at Poolewe.

heard in Lismore differed only in detail from what they had been hearing ever since the first meeting at Braes, and would continue to hear in the following months—a minute and circumstantial tale of eviction, intimidation, victimisation, imposed poverty, hunger and undernourishment. And to a large extent the Highland landlords and their spokesmen did not dispute, or attempt to answer the specific accusations levelled against them.

Unchallenged as they were, the grievances of the Highland people were to find little sympathy, when, in the spring of the following year, the Commission issued its long-awaited findings: for Napier had endeavoured to concoct a solution that would silence land agitation in the Highlands, but in a way that largely reserved the position of the landlords. The Report spoke—not surprisingly—of the Commissioners having found clear evidence of undue contraction of the areas of holding; of insecurity of tenure and the lack of compensation for improvement; of high rents and the withdrawal of the soil for the purposes of sport; and of defects in education and in the machinery of justice. But the remedies Lord Napier proposed were unacceptable to the crofters, for they did not strike anywhere near the roots of Highland landlordism. On the other hand, the Report did not please the Government or the landlords either. The Home Secretary thought that the proposals 'did not meet with acceptance in any quarter'; Lochiel did not think the Report even worth discussion; the Duke of Argyll thought it inconsistent and anomalous; and the Lord Advocate did his best to ensure that it was simply forgotten.

But while the Commission toured, and while the Government argued and delayed and manoeuvred, the people of the Highlands were taking upon themselves, in no uncertain way, the responsibility for what their rulers and masters liked to call the 'crofting problem'—if anything was wrong with the Highlands, it was in truth not so much a 'crofting problem' as a 'landlord problem'—and the landlords were soon to realise that that 'problem' was indeed a considerable one. For, as Alexander Mackenzie wrote in February, 1884, 'the real work of those who demand and will insist upon a change in the present land laws will only begin in earnest when the nature of the Report becomes known'. His prediction was soon to be justified.

The Land League

'Is it, however, not an unfortunate
fact that all Governments offer a
high premium on agitation?
The public are taught by bitter
experience that no measure of any
importance can be carried through
Parliament unless the Government of
the day is in a position to point
to a great agitation ... without
agitation experience shows that justice
shall never be done to the righteous
claims of the people.'

ALEXANDER MACKENZIE

It was in February, 1883, the month that the Government gunboat came to Glendale, that the Government finally gave way to the rising clamour of demand for a Royal Commission into crofter's grievances. Although its report, published fourteen months later, was widely criticised, and its recommendations condemned as inadequate, the tour of the Commission round the Highlands, and the great publicity and excitement attendant on it, had aroused the crofters to an intense interest in the matter of Highland land law reform. As a chairman, Napier had been conspicuously just, and had encouraged crofters to speak out and tell the truth; which, despite the ever-present fear of victimisation by the landlords, they did with passion and eloquence. The pent-up memories of generations of savage exploitation were suddenly released, the custom of submissiveness and sublimation was broken, and the conspiracy of silence smashed, as the people spoke out and told their history in the open to strangers.

The historic significance of the evidence given to the Napier Commission can hardly be exaggerated. To those who told the tale, and to their fellows who heard it, the effect was one of profound psychological liberation, at both personal and communal levels; while to the world at large the social and political conditions it exposed, and the manner of their exposure, were of no less shattering importance. Facts which had for generations lacked a means of expression were now, for the first time, articulated in public; whereas in the past statements about the Highlands had represented only the viewpoint of the Establishment, there was now the possibility of a genuine debate on the subject, though the landlords and their agents tended not to appear before Napier, but rather to make their submissions in writing and in private. Moreover, the effect of the Napier Commission was cumulative: as reports of the Commission's first hearing in Braes circulated, and as crofting tenants across the Highlands saw the truth being told there, so they were encouraged and emboldened to tell the truth about their own community. Finally the crofters in each area found it necessary to prepare for the visit of the Commission, by choosing the spokesmen and the witnesses who would go before Lord Napier; this process tended to draw them closer together, and to awaken a new political self-conciousness.

In fact, the Commission not only triggered an explosion in crofters' political self-awareness by the very act of inviting them to tell their story, but it also encouraged the emergence of the crofters as an identifiable and separate group in British society. By preparing to tell their story, by actually telling it, and by reflecting on its clear import, the crofters recognised their common interest and created an identity for themselves. And at the same time they recognised as their common enemy the Highland landlords, whose rapacity and ruthlessness was so largely responsible for the impoverished conditions of the people.

In many ways these conditions were as bad in the 1880s as they had been in previous decades. In the same week that the newly-appointed members of the Napier Commission met for the first time, it was reported that distress was severe in many areas. In Ullapool in Wester Ross, close on a thousand crofter-fishermen, impoverished by the failure of the fishing and the destruction of their crops the previous autumn, were facing starvation; and from Mull, Skye, North Uist, South Harris, Assynt and Stoer in Sutherland, there were similar reports. In Harris, conditions were as bad as they had been in the Destitution forty years before; in one district alone, over two hundred families were already hungry. Not only had the potato crop failed, but in many places the little patches of oats and barley were equally barren. On Skye, eight hundred families, perhaps as many as five thousand people, were hungry; and of Kilmuir's 460 impoverished families, 150 were actually starving. The minister of Kilmuir wrote that in a few weeks half the families would be without food, without any way of procuring food, and without even seed to put into the ground. On Mull, in Kinloch alone, thirty families were on the verge of starvation; in Gairloch, 250 people were hungry and in extreme want.

For South Harris alone, £4,000 was needed for relief purposes; for Skye, £10,000 was the minimum required; and for the Highlands as a whole, very much more was needed, and at once. Obviously the crofters themselves could not pay: even in 'normal' times, any money they saved went towards paying the rent or estate charges. As for the landlords, they were not prepared to spend their income from rents on the people who actually

Crofters' houses in North Uist. Lord Napier's official report noted, 'His habitation is usually of a character which would almost imply physical and moral degradation in the eyes of those who do not know how much decency, courtesy, virtue, and even mental refinement, survive amidst the sordid surroundings of a Highland hovel'.

produced those rents, even to save them from starvation. To be sure, they were against poverty, but not for humanitarian reasons; the reason that they condemned it (and advocated emigration for the impoverished as its remedy) was that the burden of the poor-rates fell upon themselves. For a time, indeed, the landlords of Skye were to launch their own strike, by refusing to pay these rates.

Instead, the Highland landlords asked for money from the south, so that the crofters, if they would not emigrate, might at least not be a burden to themselves, by seeking relief from the poor-fund. Thus the Earl of Dunmore visited London in March, 1883, begging money for the relief of the crofters who had (so he said) overcrowded themselves on his estates. Relief, he assured his London friends, would be given only in kind, since crofters could not be expected to know how to handle money; and at every opportunity, work would be extracted from the impoverished, for the benefit and improvement of the district. The district, of course, belonged either to Dunmore or to one of his fellow-landlords.

In response to the Earl's appeal, the Duke of Westminster kindly gave £100; on the committee of eminent gentlemen who were to distribute it, and the other lordly donations, sat none other than Lord Colin Campbell, MP, and son of the Duke of Argyll.

Against this background, then, it is little wonder that the Napier Commission was a watershed for crofter conciousness; during the course of the Commission's tour, the confidence and solidarity of the crofting population increased enormously. They could not fail to conclude from the setting up of the Commission, that whereas generations of quiescence had led merely to greater and greater hardships, the agitation in Glendale and Braes was followed almost at once by Government action. Who could tell what might result, were such agitation to be generalised right across the Highlands?

Long before the Commission arrived in any locality, the crofters there knew of its objects, its procedures, its itinerary, and its intention to visit their district. To a large extent this awareness was the work of southern spokesmen of the pro-crofter movement—John Murdoch and Alexander Mackenzie prominent among them—who toured ahead of the Commission, encouraging, organising and educating the crofters. As the Commissioners pointed out in their Report, they had all known that the progress of the Commission 'was anticipated by agents enlisted in the popular cause'. Mackenzie himself testified to Lord Napier that he had moved ahead of the Commission in the whole of Skye, and part of North Uist, in Benbecula, and in part of South Uist, and then, on the west coast, 'all along' from Thurso to Lochcarron. Murdoch, who had been sent round the Highlands by the Federation of Celtic Societies, was active too, despite slanders against him in the *Scotsman,* which accused him of complicity in Irish politics and of having taken Irish money to finance agitation. As he wrote later, he had complained to the paper repeatedly, but not a word was ever retracted; and he was 'left under that stigma and was misjudged accordingly' in different parts of the country, as he found in Assynt and the Reay country when he went there, 'to prepare the crofters for Lord Napier's Royal Commission. The only approach to a vindication which I ever got was through Sir Kenneth Mackenzie, on that Commission, asking me about the accusation ... But the *Scotsman* never withdrew its accusations, nor in any way made amends for its foul attacks on me'.

When the Napier Commission came to take its final evidence in Edinburgh and Glasgow, Murdoch appeared before it, and in a long statement endeavoured to nail the lies of the pro-landlord newspapers. At Portree, at Glendale, at Ullapool, at Inverness, and even in Edinburgh, he said, it had been alleged that the crofters had been moved and primed from without to prefer charges against factors, landlords, and others; and that thus the Royal Commission had to a large extent, been gathering, not so much the genuine testimony of the ordinary people of the Highlands, as the opinions and creations of what the landlords and their agents, especially the *Scotsman,* liked to consider 'cowardly and unscrupulous agitators'. Now it so happened that he was, from direct personal knowledge, in a position to disprove much of this allegation; and one of the best services which he could render to the Commission and to the crofters was to show how little reliance could be placed upon the claims of the *Scotsman's* implacably anti-crofter leader-writers. He had, moreover, an additional reason for setting the record straight, in that he had been mentioned as if he had, with others unknown, been engaged in getting up a fictitious case against factors and landlords, and in inciting the people to violence. The first thing to be noticed was that the landlords did not say exactly what he and his friends were supposed to have done to influence the people; 'they, as if mere sweeping assertion from one of them was enough, merely say that the delegates and those who chose them are our mouthpiece, without specifying what particular words we put into their ears or when or where we made the attempts'. It was quite clear to Murdoch that the crofters did not require to have men sent in among them from without; 'if there has been any priming in the case, the charge is to be laid at the door, not of the agitators at all, but of persons who are afraid of, and bitterly opposed to agitation'.

John Stuart Blackie, now seventy-four years old, was too old to tour with the rest ahead of Napier; but he too gave evidence to the Commission when it came to Edinburgh. His testimony was followed by that of John Mackay, who had been born, reared and educated in the parish of Rogart, Sutherlandshire, till twenty years of age; the son of a crofter, he was one of a family of nine brought up on a croft of about seven acres. Mackay had also given evidence in Golspie, as delegate for the people of the upper part of the parish of Rogart, representing the people of seventeen townships.

These four, Murdoch, Mackenzie, Blackie and Mackay, had all been prominent in the Federation of Celtic Societies, in pro-crofter journalism, and in the politics of land reform in general. Their organisational and tactical skill was of considerable value in publicising the crofter cause. But as the Napier Commission toured the Highlands, and as it deliberated and prepared its report over the winter of 1883-1884, the driving force behind the movement came less from its southern spokesmen, and more from the Highland crofters themselves. The very existence of the Napier Commission, its decision to tour widely, its practice of taking evidence in public, and the attendant publicity, had combined to produce the very effect that the Lord Advocate had feared; it had been 'the signal for increased and extended agitation'; it had, in short, opened the floodgates of a Highland land question.

Throughout 1883 and 1884, agitation spread. Before the end of 1882, forty of Lord MacDonald's tenants in Breakish had declared themselves to be on rent-strike until such time as land formerly in their possession was returned to them. The correspondent of the *Scotsman* wrote at the time that the agitation was still spreading, 'owing to the unwise counsels of outsiders, and the omission of the hitherto customary vindication of the law'. And as the grip of winter tightened, with great snowstorms and intense cold throughout the Highlands, great inroads were made into crofters' stock. In every district there were many who were absolutely destitute, having eaten the meagre potato crop, and then, in desperation, the seed for the following spring. Many had already sold all their stock to buy meal; and now that too was almost gone.

As the desperation and anger of the people became increasingly manifest, some landlords began to retreat. In Kilmuir, a 25% rent-reduction was announced; and in Shieldaig, too, there were rent-reductions. In Braes, the grazing of Ben Lee was ceded to the crofters. In the spring there was fresh talk of the men of Glendale driving the landlord's stock away from the farm of Waterstein, in defiance of the Court of Session order prohibiting them. It was reported in Portree that the people in the neighbouring townships were in a very excited state, 'and it is feared that we have not seen the worst of the affair yet'. And then the report came from Glendale: 'The horns sounded in the glen early in the afternoon; the people assembled, men and lads, and proceeding to the grazings of Waterstein, they drove off the stock that belonged to the trustees, and replaced them with stock that belongs to themselves.'

Meanwhile, in Stornoway, two thousand crofters met to consider what steps ought to be taken to bring the whole land question before the Government, 'to get the present grievances removed, and the equitable rights of the people secured to them'. The meeting, conducted in Gaelic, began with prayers and ended with the benediction; but it was with political matters that it was essentially concerned. Petitions were sent to the Prime Minister, Gladstone. The chairman of the crofters' committee had already written to Lady Matheson in London (she was shortly to sell the estate and remove herself to the south of France), informing her that the land question had so taken hold of the minds of the crofters that he now demanded that her Ladyship be good enough to instruct her factor to meet

John Stuart Blackie, who wrote 'The economical capacities of the Highlands are not to be understood by a few idle young gentlemen from the metropolis, who travel over the bare brown moors for ten days or a fortnight in the autumn, and then conceit themselves that they have seen the country'.

the committee at an early date to hear it on the subject of the grievances, and endeavour to provide a remedy; for until there was a redistribution of the land, and more grazings given to the crofters, discontent and poverty would prevail. He added that the condition of the crofters was due entirely to large possessions in the hands of sportsmen and tenant-farmers, and warned Lady Matheson that, 'if we are not to get any redress, I cannot vouch for the course the crofters of Lewis may pursue, judging from the views expressed by them at their recent meetings'.

From her fashionable London town house, Lady Matheson replied that she found it deeply offensive that he should have taken it upon himself to dare to represent the people of Lewis. She would not countenance their challenging the laws of the country, 'thus threatening their allegiance to their sovereign Queen Victoria'. As long as threats were used and seditious meetings were held she declined to allow her factor 'to hold communication with any person who, under the pleas of justice to the crofters, is endeavouring to incite and urge them to open rebellion against the Government'.

Trouble spread to Barra and to Tiree, with crofters demanding rent-reductions and the return of grazings now under the landlords' sheep. In Glendale, there was renewed trouble in March, resulting in prison sentences for five of the crofters. Across the Highlands, however, the emergent crofters' movement was not cowed by these arrests, but heartened by the defiant example of the people of Glendale. All summer, even as the Commission toured, crofters' confidence grew; and as it approached the end of its tour, trouble flared in numerous places. In the Shetlands, on the island of Foula, one of the crofters who had given evidence to Lord Napier was subjected to an attempted eviction; the whole district gathered, deforced the sheriff-officer and reinstated the crofter in his holding. In Lewis, the crofters drove the sheep of Lady Matheson's tenant-farmer from the grazings of the Melbost Links. When her Ladyship's factor returned the sheep the crofters drove them off again, and Lady Matheson appealed to the Court of Session. The crofters maintained that the grazings of the Links had been theirs until the 1850s, and made their own arrangements to contest the matter in the Court of Session.

Over the winter of 1883-84, the Commission deliberated. Lord MacDonald sojourned again in Nice; but the people of the Highlands impatiently awaited its findings. In April, when Lord MacDonald's neighbour in Kilmuir issued summons of removal against fifty crofters, the officers delivering them were summarily deforced. There was trouble in the Uists too: agitation had spread to South Uist in March, and it was reported from Lochboisdale that meetings were widely attended; flags of defiance were flying in nearly every township; and at Stoneybridge the people were threatening to seize the land. In Skye, the attitude of the crofters 'in their opposition to all constituted authority' was said in April to be 'as determined and defiant as during the last outbreak'. In defiance of a Court of Session order, Skye crofters invaded property at Leckmelm by boat, and sailed off loaded with seaweed to use as fertiliser; at once, legal proceedings were instituted. And from the island of Tiree came the report that the land question formed the chief topic of discussion on the island, and that while opinions differed as to the ultimate results of the agitation, it was generally entertained, 'that the crofters evidently now mean business. Undoubtedly much dis-satisfaction exists among the population in certain quarters, in the west end of the island principally, Moss, Ballevullin and Kilmoluag districts being those wherein disaffection is deepest'. In the Moss district no rent had been paid for some weeks past. The people there had petitioned the Duke of Argyll for a reduction in rent, which he refused to concede; he had offered some small concession, which they considered derisory; so they declined to pay any more rent. Such was the state of feeling now existing in the island, that a considerable number of the rent-striking Moss tenants had recently marched in a body to Island House to ask the factor whether one of their number had paid his rent lately. They insisted on having an answer. 'Upon receiving a negative reply, the Mossites went quietly home again, but not without making it understood that had it been otherwise the defaulter would have suffered at their hands'. Moreover, it was reported, the sheriff-officer was in real danger of serious bodily harm should he attempt the performance of his duty, and it was thus impossible for him, when legal proceedings were contemplated, to procure witnesses from amongst the islanders, 'who have been warned of the consequences attending their being a witness'. It was also said that the crofters were threatening to take forcible possession of Ben Hynish and Ben Hough as grazing-ground.

Thus 1883 and 1884 saw the spread of agitation across the Highlands, and a new element of collaboration between the crofters themselves and the largely southern-based advocates of land law reform, in the Highland Land League, or the Highland Land Law Reform Association, to give it its full title. Based at first in the south, with offices in London and Edinburgh, it very quickly won the support and the allegiance of crofters throughout the Highlands. By the spring of 1884, it was estimated that 400 to 500 crofters in Tiree alone were members, and such a level of support was not untypical. That same spring, League support in South Uist was such that the secretary and chairman of the local branch, and the secretary's father, all faced eviction from their crofts for their association with what their factor called 'rebels and unlawful men'. The summons of removal ordered these three to 'flit and remove themselves with their cattle, goods and gear, forth from their crofts and from their dwelling houses, or other premises situated therein'. The Uist men, however, chose not to remove themselves, and wrote instead to the national secretary of the League, who promised immediate publicity and assistance; it was a scenario that was to become common in the following year.

Throughout the Highlands, the people took courage at the prospect of what the League called their social emancipation; and, for their part, the authorities took fright. From police stations all over the mainland and islands came reports of disturbances, each one of them testimony to the tide of support for land law reform. On Skye, the agitation was particularly worrying: in May, 1884, the Chief Constable of Inverness wrote to Sheriff Ivory that in the previous week alone reports had arrived of meetings at Broadford, Waternish, and Fairy Bridge. In Broadford, John Mac-Pherson, one of the Glendale crofters gaoled in Edinburgh and now a leading spokesman of land law reform, addressed sixty crofters and the local minister, and 'related how he had been innocently dragged to Edinburgh, and imprisoned, through the tyranny of landlords, and the existing laws, and that the time had now arrived when the crofters should unite together and agitate their cause for freedom and more land, and by doing so that they would be sure to succeed'. At that meeting alone, fifty crofters joined the League.

Three days after the Broadford meeting, Alexander Mackay, police constable in Waternish, reported to the Chief Constable that a meeting of the League had been held by the Rev MacCallum, of Waternish, within the Established Church, Waternish, the previous Friday. The meeting was attended by about thirty of the crofters of Waternish, but none were admitted to the meeting except those who became members. 'There is a report current here today that a mass meeting of the crofters of the parishes of Duirnish, Bracadale and Snizort is to be held at Fairy Bridge on Tuesday'. Four days later, John MacPherson addressed a land reform meeting at Flashadder; that same afternoon, he and the Rev MacCallum

John MacPherson addresses a Land League meeting in Skye. The previous year he had told the Napier Commission that the landlords had given the people '...no satisfaction, but told us to have patience. We told them that our forefathers had died in good patience till now, and that we could not wait any longer—that they never got anything by their patience, but constantly getting worse'.

spoke to eight hundred men who had gathered at Fairy Bridge from the districts of Edinbane, Waternish, Dunvegan, Glendale and Bracadale.

All that month, and the following month, reports came in of Land League recruitment and agitation; and in July, Sergeant Chisholm was reporting a meeting in Fort William at which forty or fifty persons were present, principally labourers; the meeting was addressed by John MacDonald, a native of Uig, Isle of Skye, the property of Major Fraser of Kilmuir. 'A man named James Mackinnon, a native of the Island of Mull, seaman on board the SS *Nevis* of Glasgow, presently lying at Fort William pier, also addressed the meeting. Both said men spoke in strong terms against the existing land laws'.

On August 21st, Professor Blackie and Donald MacFarlane arrived by yacht at Portree. That same evening they held a meeting in the local school, whose door local supporters had smashed open earlier on, to enable them to meet there. MacFarlane was the principal speaker, his subject land law reform. He strongly urged the people to keep up the land agitation and to hold meetings so that their proceedings would be widely publicised; and he assured them that both Mr Fraser-Mackintosh and Dr Cameron, as well as himself, were ready to promote their cause, and that soon the tyranny of landlordism would be at an end. The police reported that Professor Blackie spoke next, 'strongly advising the people to keep up the agitation as hot as possible, and not to fear landlord or factor, and that he himself (at the same time flourishing his walking stick), would fight the devil if he came within his reach, and although he was getting an old man, he would not die until he would see the rights of the poor established, and the landlords done away with'.

The following month there was yet another meeting in the school hall in Portree, addressed by the Rev MacCallum, John MacPherson, and the secretary of the League's national office; this time delegates from Uist were in attendance, as well as Skyemen. The following day the same speakers addressed a meeting at Skaebost, attended by 150 crofters and (on the instructions of the Procurator Fiscal) one police agent, suitably disguised. As usual, MacCallum and MacPherson spoke in Gaelic, with MacCallum offering the benediction from the chair; and having closed the meeting, he retired 'to an unknown place' for a private meeting with local crofters' leaders. In October a hundred crofters met at Craiglea, to prepare—as the police agents reported—for the seizure of land.

Membership of the League soared, with a widespread campaign of publicity and agitation. The police in Skye grew worried at the circulation of 'seditious pamphlets' urging membership of the League, printed in Gaelic and English, and apparently emanating from London. The landlords demanded action: Fraser of Kilmuir wrote to the authorities about alarming accounts of sedition in the Highlands, and demanded police reinforcements. The Land League, he thought, was to blame. 'I hear

John MacPherson who said 'It would be as easy to stop the Atlantic Ocean as to stop the present agitation until justice has been done to the people'.

now of successive outrages, in the way of destruction of corn and peat-stacks belonging to those who do not join, whilst apparently no effort is made to interfere with those who are inciting the violence ... On the whole I think the loyal lieges should now receive a little more protection, their present position being very trying'.

When the Commission was just beginning its work, the Federation of Celtic Societies had appealed to crofters to hold meetings, public or private, without delay; to invite the Commission to visit their respective districts; to appoint the most suitable persons to give evidence; and generally to devise means by which their case would be best laid before the Commission. The Federation had appointed 'a gentleman of knowledge and experience who speaks Gaelic with fluency', to assist in this preliminary work; those requiring his advice and assistance were requested to communicate at once. It was, no doubt, to this initiative that the Earl of Dunmore was alluding in January, 1884, when he asked the Gaelic Society of Inverness, to laughter and cries of 'Rubbish!', what condemnation could be too severe for those men of the educated classes familiar with the language, who had taken advantage of it, 'to feed the flame of discontent among the ignorant and uneducated by applying the mischievous bellows of agitation'. In his opinion, the Gaelic language had never been put to a 'more unworthy and unpatriotic or wicked use than when it was employed, not as a means of tranquilising the poor people by reasoning with them in a spirit of pacification and conciliation in their own tongue, but, on the contrary, in urging them to rebellion and crime'.

The Federation had issued its appeal in May 1883; that same month, the Glendale men were released from the Calton Gaol in Edinburgh. On leaving the gaol, at eight in the morning, John MacPherson was escorted by pipers to the station. He proceeded to Queen Street Station in Glasgow, where he addressed a crowd of supporters and well-wishers in Gaelic from his carriage window: and thence to Strome Ferry and Portree in order to appear as a witness before the Royal Commission. It was reported that the train moved out of the station amid loud cheers, much waving of hats, and shouts of 'the land for the people'.

All summer MacPherson was active in the agitation; in August, he spoke in Fraserburgh to almost two thousand Highlanders who were there for the summer fishing. The following month, it was reported from Glendale that 'the prospects look very bad indeed. The coming home of the East Coast fishermen is anticipated with fond desire by parents and wives, though it is believed a good many will stay away owing to the unsuccessful state of the season'. But of those who did return, many were at once drawn into the agitation; and in December, MacPherson, as president of the newly-formed Glendale branch of the League, convened its first meeting in the local school-house. In the New Year the agitation spread further to hitherto unaffected areas; in Dunvegan five hundred men walked on a black February night to form their local branch of the League. The *Oban Times* reported that 'branch societies of this new mode of agitating crofters' grievances are now in full swing'; and already the national office of the League listed branches throughout Skye, Ross-shire, Caithness, and the Outer Islands.

By the spring, further new branches of the League had sprung up all over the Highlands; in Mull, for example, February saw the formation of the Creich branch, complete with office-bearers and a campaign for membership. Meanwhile, nationally, under the presidency of Donald MacFarlane, the League was demanding such changes in the land laws as would secure fair rents, security of tenure, compensation for improvement, 'and such an apportionment of the land as will promote the welfare of the people'. Henry George, the internationally known land-reformer, visited the Highland community in Greenock with John Murdoch, and noted that he 'entered the town as if I had been a hero fresh from the Egyptian campaigns. As it was in Greenock, so was it more or less in all the large towns of Scotland ... An active propaganda is being carried into the Highlands'. The League sent one of its members on a speaking tour of Skye; arrangements were made for him to lecture in Dunvegan, Waternish, Glendale, Valtos, Uig, Portree and Braes. John MacPherson was now a full-time organiser for the League; the *Oban Times* reported: 'The movement is carried on with almost incredible enthusiasm and determination. Meetings are being held at regular intervals, and speeches delivered by crofters that would do credit to an MP'.

From all quarters came reports of the success of the agitation— from Barra, from Strath, from Loch Eport, from Loch Alsh, from Portree, from Lewis, and all over the mainland. In June it was reported that the League now had scores of branches and many thousands of members; and many more had joined by September. By then, John MacPherson had been touring in Argyll for a month, and branches had been formed at Easdale, Salen, Tobermory, Bunessan, Iona, Tiree, Lismore, Lochaline, Strontian, Ardnamurchan, Taynuilt and Oban. MacPherson addressed the Tiree branch on August 25th; and with resolutions in favour of giving the vote to crofters and the teaching of Gaelic in Highland schools, two delegates were appointed to attend a conference of crofters' representatives from all parts, which was shortly to be held in Dingwall. In Strontian, that same day, the branch meeting conducted similar business, and demanded that Parliament give ordinary men the right to vote—a resolution which the Trades Union Congress was to echo at its meeting in Aberdeen the following week. At MacPherson's meeting in Easdale, four hundred turned out to hear him speak; feeling was running high, for Blackie and Donald MacFarlane, MP, were expected to arrive by sea in Oban at any time. At the Lochaline meeting, a hundred men were present; this was a very large turnout for such a sparsely populated district; but interest was heightened by the imminence of a mass land-law reform demonstration, timed to coincide with the crofters' conference in Dingwall the following month, which Blackie, Fraser-Mackintosh and Charles Cameron were expected to attend. Luing now had a branch; and, when the question was put, at its introductory meeting, the whole audience showed its readiness to join the League. In Salen, where a hundred men attended the meeting, almost every man present agreed to become a member. In Lismore, in the chapel at Bachuil, it was reported that, on a motion being put to the meeting for a show of hands on the side of the League, all hands were up in an instant. From Barra it was reported that their recent visitors, Mr MacFarlane and Professor Blackie, were held everywhere on the island in the greatest esteem. At Unst in Shetland, hundreds of fishermen met to demand land reform; many of them were crofters from Skye, Lewis, Caithness, Sutherland and Argyll, presently engaged in the herring fishing there. From Iona came the report that a branch association had already been formed there; most of the householders were already members, 'and those who had not previously joined intimated their intention of doing so at once, so that these districts may be considered as rapidly ripening for the great struggle'. The Kilbrandon branch sent a petition to Gladstone in August. In Strontian, at a meeting to form a local branch, 'a large proportion of those present forthwith enrolled'; at Lochaline, the same motion was accepted unanimously. The Aberdeen branch was demanding changes in the land laws, giving the people more land at a fair rent, with secure tenure and compensation for improvement. In Kilchoan, a large audience assembled at very short notice to hear MacPherson, who was repeatedly asked to return, so that those who had not known of his coming might also hear him.

Across the Highlands the pattern was the same, the demands identical, the support immense. At the Stenscholl branch meeting in Skye, Hugh Matheson impressed upon the members the need for united and earnest perseverance in pursuit of reform, and denounced any crofter who would not support the movement, saying that such men could often be seen in the kitchens of their oppressors. 'selling their birthright for scraps from their landlord's table'. Matheson insisted that 'landlord' was a false title, there being no absolute lord of the land 'but the One Almighty Creator who made the land'. He believed that the land was meant to belong to the people, and he wondered how landlords could dare, 'like so many gods', to say that the land was theirs, and that they could dispose of it according to their pleasure. The fish that was yesterday miles away from the land was claimed by the landlord the moment it neared the shore, and so also were the birds of the air as soon as they flew over his land. The law made it so, said Matheson, because landlords were themselves the lawmakers, and it was a wonder any poor man was allowed to breathe the air of heaven and drink from the mountain stream, without having the factors and the police pursuing him as a thief.

At the same meeting Norman Stewart concurred, in saying that the people had suffered too long and too patiently; but he noted that 'a cloud of relief, at first no bigger than a man's hand, has appeared, and is rapidly growing larger'. Let them make their grievances loudly and widely known. They knew that all good men were on their side, 'but we must agitate more loudly and more unitedly still, so that our cause may become still more widely known, and will yet triumph, and we shall receive justice'. Ronald Maclean proposed that henceforth every crofter should refuse to do any work for any landlord or factor, thus throwing them in a 'rather awkward fix'; and that the crofters should independently revalue the land let to them and pay to the landlord not a penny more than that valuation. And Murdo Nicolson told the meeting of how his factor had offered him the sum of £3 if he would but leave the League, and of how he had replied that he would not give up his connection with the movement until they got their grievances redressed, 'even if I had to sell my very clothes'.

The spirit of that branch meeting in Stenscholl was typical of many; as it was reported, all the speeches were enthusiastically cheered throughout, while there were interruptions of 'a very uncomplimentary nature against the lairds, factors and tacksmen. This is a fair specimen of what is going on in almost every township in the west'. In August, a parliamentary election in Ross and Cromarty was contested for the first time in thirty-two years, when the Establishment's nominee was challenged by an advocate of land law reform. Naturally, the landlords won by a handsome margin, because of the restricted franchise; for in that by-election only 1,720 people in the whole county were entitled to vote. Nevertheless, the very possibility of a land reform candidate was previously inconceivable; and for the people of Ross, even if they could not vote for him, his presence was more than symbolic. The new member for Ross-shire was just 24 years old, but owned 15,000 acres in the county, and was already deputy-lieutenant for Fife. He sported three addresses; his father had also been an MP and a colonel in the army; and his grandfather had been none other than Sir Hector Munro of Novar, a clearing landlord of the previous century. Sir James Matheson had held the seat unopposed for sixteen years, and his successor, Alexander Matheson for a similar period; young Ronald Craufurd Munro Ferguson of Novar, however, was to hold the seat for no more than that number of months. In fact it was but a sign of the times that there had been a land law reform candidate in the contest; for despite the implacable opposition of the House of Lords, the Government was preparing to extend the franchise; moreover, and with an eye to the newly created popular vote in places like the Highlands, it was preparing to legislate on land law. Within a month of his selection, the new member for Ross and Cromarty was to join Gladstone on the platform of Edinburgh's Corn Exchange Hall, and hear him tell 4,000 supporters that it was the deep conviction of the members of his Government that, when they could find the time and opportunity, 'it will be their duty to give their most serious and sympathetic attention to the question which has been brought before them, in a manner so lucid, by the labours of the Commission over which Lord Napier presided'.

The Government having thus declared itself ready to legislate on the Highland land question, a further impetus was to come from the crofters themselves. The day before Gladstone's appearance in Edinburgh, a League branch was formed in Oban with the Reverend Donald M'Caig of Muckairn in the chair and John MacPherson of Glendale as the main speaker; resolutions were passed demanding land law reform and the extension of the franchise to the crofters. No fewer than 1,000 crofters had

84

walked in from outlying districts to express support, in Argyll Square, for the right to vote and determine the laws under which they lived. The following day, the demand for reform of the franchise laws was reiterated in Wick, when 10,000 joined a demonstration and rally there.

The following Tuesday, just three days after Gladstone's tumultuous reception in Edinburgh, members and associations and branches of the League from throughout the country attended another meeting, smaller and in a lesser city, but no less significant for the crofters of the Highlands, when they met for their first national conference in the town of Dingwall. Delegates came from the county associations in Ross, Inverness, Argyll and Sutherland, as well as from the Edinburgh and London branches. The Scottish Farmers' Alliance had a delegation present; the Scottish Land Restoration League had sent its representative, Mr Shaw-Maxwell. The crofters' delegates were there, too, from every part of the Highlands—from the branches in Lewis, Halladale, Strathy, Forres, Grantown, Lochalsh, Kilmuir, Culbokie, Resolis, Evanton and Caithness, and many more. The list of individuals who had given notice of their intention to attend ran like a roll-call of land reform organisers—Professor Blackie; Charles Fraser-Mackintosh, MP, and Charles Cameron, MP; Dr Clarke, the land law reform candidate in the Ross-shire bye-election; Donald Murray, Ross-shire born and Gaelic speaking secretary of the London office of the League; Dugald Cowan, secretary of the Edinburgh office; Alexander Mackenzie of Inverness, John MacPherson of Glendale and Angus Sutherland of Glasgow. Among the speakers at the conference that day were Donald Murray, John MacPherson, John Mackay of Hereford, Donald MacFarlane, MP, Alexander Mackenzie, the Rev Cumming of Melness, Neil MacNeil of Tiree, and Michael Buchanan of Barra. Delegates who heard them speak, some in English and some in Gaelic, had come by boat, train and foot, from places like Inverness, Farr, Strathspey, Skye, Rogart, Alness, Lochalsh, Kintail, Strathpeffer, Gairloch, North and South Uist and the Orkneys.

The conference expressed approval of Gladstone's comments in the Corn Hall on the previous Saturday; but it was with more immediate issues that it was principally concerned. It discussed the report of the Napier Commission, which it considered inadequate; it demanded a Land Court with the power to fix rents and with judicial and administrative functions for the crofting areas; and it insisted that any legislation should provide for security of tenure on the basis of Land Court rents. The conference called for the compulsory enlargement of the land available to the crofting townships, and demanded amendments in the crofters' favour with reference to deer-forests, whether established or proposed, and with reference to the Game Laws. It was agreed to establish a land reform newspaper for circulation in the Highlands; the committee charged with responsibility for the paper included Mackenzie, John Mackay, Donald Murray, Dr Clarke, Dugald Cowan, and delegates from Lochalsh and Dingwall.

On the following day thousands joined the League's demonstration through Dingwall; and at the concluding rally, the demands of the conference were endorsed overwhelmingly. At the rally, Donald MacFarlane, Fraser-Mackintosh, and the Reverend Donald MacCallum of Waternish formally proposed the rally's support for the Land League, 'in its efforts to effect such changes in the land laws as will secure to the Highland people the right to live on their native soil'; of the thousands present, not one voice was raised in dissent.

But the most significant policy adopted by the conference and rally pertained to carrying the crofters' cause into Parliament. At an evening meeting following the conference, Mackenzie had proposed a motion, which had been unanimously accepted, to the effect that the question of land law reform be made a test one at the next election, and that a committee be formed to choose candidates to contest the Highland parliamentary constituencies in the cause of land law reform. And at the rally, under Professor Blackie's chairmanship, Mackenzie moved that the meeting express its approval of the Franchise Bill, introduced by Gladstone, and passed by the House of Commons; and that it affirm its opinion that the power of veto possessed by the Lords was productive of much mischief when exercised in opposition to the deliberate will of the people; with the recommendation of such constitutional changes as would make the Lords' veto inoperative for the future. Again, not a voice was raised in protest; and it only remained for Shaw-Maxwell and the Rev Cumming of Melness to complete the matter by proposing, without opposition, that the meeting pledge itself to use its utmost power and influence to secure the return to Parliament, 'of such men only as are known to be in full and thorough sympathy with the people on the great social question of land law reform'.

The rally broke up; the delegates returned home with news, views, reports, policies, even greater confidence; the new committees began to plan membership drives, the launching of the newspaper, and the campaign for parliamentary representation. It was but ten years since the arrest and trial of the men from Bernera; and as the delegates from the island branches made their way home by Fort William and Oban, or down the line to Strome Ferry and thence by boat, many must have wondered at, and rejoiced in, the successes of the crofters in that decade. As the *Celtic Magazine* had forecast, the conference itself was of historic importance, and ushered in a new phase in the history of the movement; and that movement, daily stronger and more confident, was on the offensive.

Offensive in a different sense it was to the propertied rich, who responded with a mixture of mocking contempt and serious alarm. The Dingwall policy programme they termed impossible, fomented by agitators, unrepresentative of the wishes of the crofters, an outrageous infringement on the rights of private property and the interests of sound estate management. The *Edinburgh Courant* proclaimed in a leader that 'it is unjust in the extreme to constitute any court an arbiter between landlord and tenant with regard to the price to be paid for the use of land'; but it did not locate or define this injustice; and it ignored the fact that the Court of

Session and sundry Highland sheriff courts had for generations repeatedly arbitrated—in practice—between landlord and tenant with regard to the use of the land. The *Times* of London characterised the whole proceedings as a piece of pernicious nonsense, and could 'anticipate nothing but mischief from a policy of public agitation'. The *Scotsman* thought the crofters' leaders to be carpet-baggers, either under-educated—in which case they should keep their place—or over-educated, in which case they were to be condemned for failing to join the *Scotsman* in keeping the rest in their place.

Such advice, however, could do nothing to still the demand among crofters for a thoroughgoing land reform. The Royal Commission had made a serious national issue of the Highland land question, not least in the areas most affected by that question. Crofter resistance was now a matter of everyday occurrence, and there could be no return to the blinkered passivity of earlier days. Yet the Government still shrank from infringing the property rights of the landowners by returning land to the people; instead, it determined to attempt once more to close the flood-gates of agitation, and crush popular resistance, by resort to military force.

The agitation spreads

*'The arguments against deer-forests
are unanswerable. What would be
said in England if one or two
Scotchmen and Americans were to
buy up the whole of Lancashire,
turn out the population, and make
of it a deer-park? The thing would
surely not be tolerated.'*

J A CAMERON

The second week of January, 1885, was a busy one for Donald Cameron of Lochiel. For months, his main aim had been to organise Highland landlord opinion and steer it to a position which would enable the land agitation to be concluded on terms most favourable to themselves. For weeks, he had been in urgent contact with the Home Secretary, attempting to manufacture a compromise solution that would silence the League, and yet leave the material interests of the Highland landlords substantially unharmed. In December he had written to Harcourt, the Home Secretary, offering observations on the best means of restoring confidence and tranquillity in those districts where agitation was 'unhappily now prevalent'. There seemed to him to be a general desire, among owners of land in the Highlands, to come to terms with their crofting tenants. He had been corresponding with some and talking to others. 'As you know,' he wrote, 'a few of us, and not the least influential, met in London, and were unanimous in the determination to recommend to the favourable consideration of northern proprietors certain bases of concession, calculated, as we think, to meet to a large extent the demand on the part of the crofters.' Lochiel went on to argue against legislation, with its element of compulsion, and argued instead for a policy of voluntary landlord concession. In places situated as the Hebrides were, nothing could guarantee the rent due to the landlord should an agitation or strike develop—not even a 'fair rent' determined by legislation. How much better would be 'a voluntary arrangement which would offer less chance of "strikes", and the dispatch of marines', argued Lochiel.

Harcourt sent Lochiel's long letter to the strongly anti-crofter Lord Advocate; he too favoured voluntary action, replying to Harcourt that he believed that the Highland proprietors were generally actuated by the 'most kindly feelings and the most benevolent intentions' towards their poor tenants; and that 'now that their personal attention has been called to the condition of many of these tenants', the fullest reliance could be placed upon these proprietors generally making 'just and even generous' concessions to them. But the Lord Advocate feared that it was now too late to avoid at least a measure of legislation, and indeed that it was now too late to buy-off the crofters' movement for anything less than the price it demanded. Harcourt had already appealed to the landlords, in a speech in the House of Commons, urging them to do something to silence the agitation; and Lochiel himself had convened meetings of landlords in London, both at the Home Office and at the Lord Advocate's residence, impressing on them the need to devise a settlement that would save the Highland landlord from expropriation and extinction.

Then, on the evening of Tuesday, 13th January, in the Station Hotel in Inverness, Lochiel addressed the Inverness Gaelic Society, impressing on his audience the urgency with which he and his fellow-landlords desired a 'settlement' and explaining that only the intransigence of the crofters stood in the way of a 'settlement' that would find favour with landlords like himself. He had hard words for Charles Cameron, Donald MacFarlane,

90

Fraser-Mackintosh, and John MacPherson; but most of all, Lochiel condemned the rent-strike, proclaiming it to be dishonest, and fatal to the best interests of the crofters. Lochiel concluded his remarks by urging his listeners each to exert himself to the utmost to rescue crofters from the influence of evil counsellors and also, perhaps to the surprise of his audience, 'to assist in removing the grievances under which they have so long suffered'. That night he apologised for raising such a matter; but in his report to Harcourt, he expressed satisfaction at the manner in which he had used his platform at the Gaelic Society to publicise the landlords' case, and took pains to tell the Home Secretary that his speech had been 'warmly received'.

The following day Lochiel continued his search for what he described as a settlement. By two o'clock in the afternoon, and largely through Lochiel's efforts, there had foregathered in the Caledonian Hotel representatives of almost fifty Highland estates. They were there for the Inverness Proprietors' Conference, assembled (in the words of the circular inviting them there) 'with the object of taking into consideration the invitation made to them by the Home Secretary to endeavour to accede to the reasonable wishes of their tenantry so far as it lies in their power to do so'. Lochiel had invited many of the greatest Highland landlords—men and women who between them had owned and controlled both Highlands and Highlanders for generations. For such as these, it was an endeavour of no small magnitude to consider even the smallest accession to the demands of mere crofting tenants; and the identity of the participants strongly suggested that, whatever the conference might propose, it would not be inimical to the interests of the landlords, or favourable to the interests of the people. The Duke of Sutherland, who had been intended as chairman of the gathering, had not appeared; he had, however, despatched his son, the Marquis of Stafford, to represent him, and to preside over the meeting. Under his presidency, and in closed and secret debate, the landlords and their deputising factors and agents discussed the matter; among them were Lord Lovat, Munro Ferguson of Novar, Major Fraser of Kilmuir, Astley-Nicholson of Arisaig, Sir Kenneth MacKenzie, and many others from Cromarty, Ross, Skye, Sutherland, and Lewis. There had also been preliminary meetings of smaller groups, in London and at Lord Lovat's nearby seat, Beaufort Castle. At the conference Lord MacDonald was represented by the factor for his Skye estates; Lady Matheson sent her chamberlain, who had also attended the pre-conference meetings in London. The Duke of Argyll, perhaps the greatest enemy of the crofters' movement, was also absent; but he had, as Lord Napier later reported, been an influential adviser to the pre-conference discussions.

After three hours of heated debate, during which the proprietors from the islands pressed for state aid to help remove their crofting tenants to the colonies, the meeting unanimously adopted a set of proposals regarding which Harcourt was shortly to write to the Prime Minister: 'This is certainly a great step to have gained. This flag of truce ought to remove (I wish I could say I thought it would remove) the asperity of class feeling.' The *Scotsman,* anti-crofter as ever, speculated hopefully that, in all likelihood, the meeting at Inverness would have the effect of lessening the influence of the outside agitators; for 'violent accusations have been made against the proprietors, but it has never been shown that they were, as a body, indifferent to the welfare of the people who held land under them.'

Both Harcourt and the *Scotsman* were wrong. At the meeting the landlords, though certainly worried, were even now unwilling to make real concessions to the demands of the crofters' movement; as Lochiel told the Lord Advocate, there had been great difficulty in getting the conference to agree to the resolutions formulated at the pre-conference meetings, and the conference had almost broken down on occasions. Consequently, all that it offered, in effect, was a reminder to the Government that the landlords still considered emigration to be a remedy; the complaint that they themselves paid too much in rates; an offer of leases to crofters not in arrears with rent; and a resolution to offer to crofters an 'undertaking' to increase the size of their holdings, 'as suitable opportunities offer, and where the crofters are in a position profitably to occupy and stock the same.' As Lord Napier pointed out, the Inverness proposals contained no absolute security for the preservation of the existing crofting areas, no provisions for township improvements, and no restriction on the future formation of deer-forests; as he put it, somewhat acidly, 'a large measure of concession could not, perhaps have been secured in connection with unanimous assent'.

The *Times* of London opined that the general belief now was that crofters would not be satisfied with any concessions made by proprietors, and that they would carry on the land agitation until their demands were conceded. The *Times* was correct: the proposals from the Inverness Proprietors' Conference merely induced anger, derision, and a strengthening of collective resolve on the part of the crofters. Within a week, the people of Braes met to discuss the landlords' proposals, and resolved to accept no concessions that they might offer, but to continue to press for legislation that would recognise their demands as rights in law. They unanimously rejected the Inverness proposals as quite worthless, and declared that men must live on their own native land, and that deer-forests and sheep-farms must be divided among the crofters. The *Oban Times,* whose editor had addressed the meeting at Braes, interpreted the offer of concessions as a sure sign that the landlords were on their knees; and Donald MacFarlane wrote that 'the action was too late and too insufficient.' Just two years before, the Highland proprietors had denied that the people had any wrongs to complain of; they had said that there was no remedy but emigration. 'And now, at a most influential meeting, they practically admit all they have denied ... Is it possible that two years ago they were ignorant of all these things?' Agitation had been denounced and 'agitators' had been slandered, 'but if it was not the horn of agitation that summoned this meeting what else was it?' The people were on strike and their masters had found the present a suitable opportunity for making promises, because an agitation was on foot that could not be quelled by police or marines, or threats of factors, or notices of removal. 'The small cloud that rose in the Highlands little more than two years ago will not be dispelled by the signs of alarmed lairds at Inverness. It is rolling southwards, and its shadow, like an eclipse, is visible over the whole kingdom.'

In Lochcarron, a packed meeting of crofters expressed itself dissatisfied with any voluntary concession on the part of the proprietors unless it were secured by law; 'it was further recommended that the agitation be kept up'. The day following the Inverness conference, the crofters of Glendale, forbidden from the halls of their church and school, met outside in the snow to hear the Rev MacCallum, John MacPherson, and Duncan Cameron of Oban tell them to keep firmly on their course, and 'not yield one jot.' Let them not give up the agitation, 'for all these promises of lairds and factors', until they had legislation on the question. The League circulated the crofting counties urging opposition to any moves to accept or give credence to the Inverness proposals; from Glendale a letter was sent to Gladstone, saying that the people there had heard of a landlords' meeting being held in Inverness behind closed doors, 'where evidently an explosive plot has been schemed'; as to the resolutions said to have been passed at this secret conference, they looked upon them as a scheme to blind both the crofters and the Government, 'in order to leave the present iniquitous land laws unaltered, with the view of preserving to themselves the power of doing in the future what they have done in the past'.

Within a week of the Proprietors' Conference 1,200 people met in Glasgow, in the City Halls, under the auspices of the anti-landlord movement. Henry George, the Rev MacCallum, Shaw-Maxwell, and John Murdoch, were present; John MacPherson sent his apologies for being unable to attend. Murdoch told the meeting that the concessions made by the landlords at their recent conference showed that they were already on their knees. In the Highlands as a whole, this was the commonest reaction to the conference. At many of the crofters' meetings the response to the landlords' suggestion of leases was a stern refusal even to consider them, since doing so would imply acceptance of the right of the landlord to dispose of the earth, whereas they believed the land to belong to those who worked it. What use was the offer of a lease to those not in arrears, when, throughout the Highlands, crofters who were not in arrears because of rack-renting were in arrears because of rent-strike? Charles Cameron's *North British Daily Mail* put the crofters' viewpoint in a blunt paragraph; the lairds had to face the inevitable and make the best of it—what was there for them now to do, but to band themselves together, and try to bring about some compromise? But they should have tried that two years ago; it was too late now; they had prejudiced their case 'by a long resistance of justice; and in the end, and that soon, as they now perceive, it is justice that will triumph.'

But of all the commentaries on the proposals of the Inverness conference, the most scathing was that of Alexander Mackenzie, the Ross-shire crofter's son who was editor of the *Celtic Magazine*. 'The more we consider these resolutions,' he wrote, 'the more we are impressed with their worthlessness, except insofar as they may be held to be a confession that something must be done, or the days of landlordism, on its present footing, are already numbered. No sensible person, however, in the least acquainted with the ideas, past conduct, and the oblivious short-sightedness hitherto exhibited by landlords generally, and more especially Highland landlords, could expect any reasonable concession from a meeting composed as the Inverness meeting was composed.' The resolutions were at least two years too late. The time for voluntary concessions was past, and the actions of the landlords at Inverness would serve no good purpose, except for the fact that the conference had been a wonderful exhibition of the true colours of landlordism. Anyone who thought that mere tinkering would now suffice was living in a fool's paradise. 'We have no hesitation,' MacKenzie wrote, 'in saying that nothing short of the ... compulsory re-settlement of the people on the best portions of their native land, from which they have, in the past, been so harshly removed, will have this effect. Holding this opinion, as we very firmly do, it would be a waste of space to discuss the Inverness resolutions, beyond pointing out that they present the Highland proprietors on their knees, confessing their sins, and in this way effectually discouraging any possible opposition on their part to such legislative changes as will make the Highland people quite independent of the landlordism of the future.'

If the landlords were on their knees, the Highland crofters' movement was very firmly on its feet—organised, informed and confident. Since the Dingwall conference membership of the League had continued to grow spectacularly. In 1882, Mackenzie had been chosen secretary of the newly-formed Inverness branch of the League; the circular issued over his signature claimed for the new association that the sole requirement to make it a real power for good was that all who believed in its objects should at once enrol themselves among its members. And the crofters did enrol themselves in the League, enthusiastically and in large numbers. Within a year of the September conference in Dingwall, the League boasted 160 branches and at least 15,000 members at a national level, with very many more members at the local level. In the crofting areas support for the movement was universal. By the time of the Proprietors' Conference, the rent-strike in Skye was well under way and spreading daily. At a League meeting in Glendale, the day after the Conference, the crofters laughed and cheered as Duncan Cameron remarked, anent the landlords' proposed concessions on rent, that they were not in much of a position to offer anything on rents, since not many had been paid recently, and even less were going to be paid in the future. The Government was shortly to send to the north its own secret agent, one MacNeill, to report on the political condition of the Highlands; from Skye, MacNeill was to report that 'the teachings of the Land League seem to have penetrated to every district'. In his estimation, every man of the crofter and cottar classes, with many merchants and artisans besides, was an enrolled member. Whether from sympathy with the League's objectives, a desire to maintain relations with their neighbours, or perhaps from fear of outrage, he did not know, but open dissentients were now rare, and even those who still professed independence were secretly anticipating a future when the landlords would be forever gone from the island.

From the Uists, Harris and Barra, the news was similar. The individuals occupied in arousing agitation were 'the same whose names occur so frequently' on the other side of the Minch—the Rev Donald MacCallum, Alexander Mackenzie and John MacPherson. John Murdoch, too, had been for some years an annual visitor to South Uist. The doctrines preached by these persons were all but universally accepted in Barra. As to the other islands, the mass of the population were fully in sympathy with the movement. 'The truth I believe to be that Land Leagueing is as popular in Harris and North Uist as in Barra, but that the latter island enjoys the services of a specially active local secretary, who is privately encouraged by the resident Roman Catholic clergyman ... and thus the population of South Uist are probably prepared for mischief when opportunity occurs, as also those of Benbecula'.

MacNeill's report on Lewis was especially alarming. He had, as he wrote to the Secretary of State, conferred with Mr William MacKay, chamberlain to Lady Matheson, whose information was accurate and ample, and, by his advice, he abstained from disclosing the object of his visit to any other permanent resident. The facts disclosed by Mr MacKay were so important that he could not delay to make the Minister aware of them. All the cottars and crofters in Lewis, including those belonging to the Naval Reserve, were members of the League. The first emissaries who visited the district seemed to have been Messrs Murdoch (late of the *Highlander*) and Mackenzie (of the *Celtic Magazine*); but early in 1883 a public meeting had been held under the presidency of the Rev Angus McIver, minister of Uig, and a Mr MacMillan, Free Church minister at Ullapool. 'The next public meeting was held in October 1884, when Messrs McIver, MacCallum (Waternish), MacPherson (Glendale), and several local agitators were present. Outrages have been numerous ... I am led to the conclusion that it is the deliberate intention of the people to deprive Lady Matheson of the whole revenue hitherto derived from sporting rents'.

As for the mainland, though MacNeill thought the movement less strong there than in the islands, in part because of a recent hardening of opinion against it on the part of many Free Church ministers, he reckoned nevertheless that it had gained a firm hold of the people in Sutherlandshire, Ardnamurchan, Tiree, and some parts of Mull. There seemed to be hardly a parish on the coast which had not been visited by 'the same active emissaries' whose names occurred so frequently in the islands, Messrs MacCallum, Mackenzie and John MacPherson. In the district of the

Island of Mull, so MacNeill reported, the movement was strong in the Ross of Mull, and in Iona, with influential branches at Salen and Dervaig. In Ardnamurchan, in the western part of the peninsula, 'the whole population belongs, and forms one of the centres of its greatest activity'. MacNeill thought that the strength of the movement in Ardnamurchan was due to the presence of a brother of Donald MacCallum as minister in neighbouring Strontian. Not many miles to the north of Strontian, in Arisaig, where the crofters' evidence before the Napier Commission had been largely given by Donald MacCallum himself (who was still minister there at that time), the head stalker to Lord Kilcoursie explained that the great bulk of the population were in sympathy with the movement. 'The first agitators here were the Rev Donald MacCallum (now of Waternish), and Mr Eneas Macdonnell of Morar. Mr Murdoch was also here, and Mr Alexander Mackenzie of Inverness. Mr Macdonnell, of Morar, has since carried on the agitation, and in his absence, Andrew Macdonald, a tailor in South Morar'. The Arisaig doctor informed MacNeill that: 'It may be said that every man of the crofter and cottar class is a Land Leaguer— either actually a member, or in sympathy with the League ... The Rev Donald MacCallum (now of Waternish, then minister here) was the first agent of the League; Mr Murdoch was also here; but, except the *Oban Times,* no incendiary literature was circulated. There was no need of coercion, as the sympathy was general ...; it is certain that some of the Catholic clergy in this district are the most violent supporters of the Land League'.

As it was in Ardnamurchan and in Arisaig, so it was to the north, among the hills and the sea-lochs of the western seaboard. The Duchess of Sutherland's sub-factor at Ullapool reported that the people of the Loch Broom area were thoroughly imbued with the principles of the League, and believed that the land should be, and would be, distributed among them; in short, they thought that the land was justly theirs, and that the exaction of rent was an unjust act. The Free Church clergy had been the original propagators of these doctrines, but they had lately held aloof 'as if in pursuance of some general resolution or arrangement' among themselves. Extreme newspapers were also circulated in the district, the sub-factor complained. From the same town, the police sergeant reported that the whole population was in sympathy with the movement; strong support was also reported in the districts of Inverewe and Gruinard Bay; in Gairloch, 'the League has a strong hold of the people, and numbers probably 150 enrolled members, with a regular organisation, a chairman, and a secretary ... Mr Alexander Mackenzie, of Inverness, was the first to bring Land League teaching here; and being a native of the parish, he was listened to. John MacPherson (Glendale) also addressed a meeting, and advised "no-rent".'

From Applecross, the local minister reported that 'there is a regular Land League organisation, with president and secretary ... There was, and is, a good deal of sympathy with Land League doctrines'; while of Lochcarron it was alleged that 'practically the whole crofter and cottar population are Land League'. From Lochinver, the wife of the local Free Church minister reported that 'the Land League has complete hold of the people in Sutherlandshire', and she knew of hardly any exceptions among her neighbours. The minister himself maintained that 'the League has great hold of the people', and reported that he, in common with his colleagues generally, had been obliged to discontinue his attendance at meetings because of the extreme views which were now being expressed. The Lochinver constable stated that 'the Land League is universally favoured by crofters and cottars throughout the country ... there is a considerable circulation of Land League literature, both newspapers and leaflets, which impress on the people that they have a right to the land'.

And in the weeks and months following the Dingwall conference, inspired by the fervent belief that they did have a right to the land, ever-increasing numbers of crofters began quite simply to repossess the Highlands. Scarcely was the conference concluded, when the crofters in South Uist were in conflict with Lady Gordon Cathcart. At Grogary, one of her Ladyship's fields was seized forcibly by the crofters, who drove her cattle away and replaced them with their own stock. Moreover, 'an attempt was made to waylay Mr Maclennan, the factor on the estate, and he only escaped injury by friendly warning'. A week later, there were reports of another 'most malicious outrage': entry had been gained to the Church via a vestry window, and the interior sprayed with paraffin as a welcome for her Ladyship, who was to attend service on the following morning.

The week after the Dingwall conference, Donald MacFarlane had arrived by yacht at Tiree, and had convened a 'monster meeting' of crofters at Baugh. At anchor in Gott Bay, he had been met by Neill MacNeill, delegate from the crofters in the east of the island, who was also expecting the arrival of John MacPherson of Glendale that same day. The following week, with feeling running high throughout the Highlands, the Rev MacCallum and MacPherson were touring Benbecula, South Uist and Barra. At Stoneybridge, the speakers were met by pipers and flag-waving supporters. Cases of arson and intimidation under the cover of darkness were occurring with increasing frequency. As for Skye, the *Oban Telegraph* reported, towards the end of the same month, that the centres of agitation were at Glendale in the parish of Duirinish, and at Eastside in Kilmuir. To all appearances, the agitation was becoming intensified, and still spreading; deeds had been done with impunity, for some time back, which would not be tolerated for a day in other parts of the country— deeds of malice and lawlessness. 'And since so many officers of the law have been thrashed and beaten in these districts with impunity, no hope of enforcing legal actions can be seriously entertained, and it is becoming proverbial that "there is no law in Skye".' The same report noted that many acts of shameful mischief had recently been committed in South Uist; 'the outlook now is most discouraging'. By the end of September it was reported that the League was operating vigorously in Mull, too; at Salen and at other centres of population, it had created a hitherto unknown pitch of interest and excitement on the land question: 'fuel has undoubtedly been heaped upon a smouldering fire, and if proper remedies are not forthcoming, it will burst with volcanic fierceness over the length and breadth of the Highlands'.

In October, the men from Iochdar in South Uist expropriated yet another of Lady Cathcart's fields; in Kilmuir, the crofters resolved to withhold payment of rent, and to subscribe to a legal fund for their defence in the event of legal proceedings being taken against them. This move was agreed on unanimously, as was the decision henceforth to boycott both the factor and his assistants; and it was made known that any crofter who chose not to support the League would be inviting the destruction of his property. From Lewis came a report that 'the land agitation has reached a very acute and critical stage'. In the parish of Uig, the crofters of practically every township were on rent-strike, and though the factor had toured for a week, attempting to collect the rents, he had returned home without a penny. By mid-October, land-seizure was common practice in Uig, the crofters having forcibly taken possession of the holdings of the large farmers and refusing even to meet with authorities for discussion regarding the seizures. The correspondent of the *Oban Telegraph* wrote that 'respect for law and order has for some time past been at a discount in the island; but the open and avowed renunciation of all authority and government which now prevails is only of recent date, and is traceable to the bad advice of unprincipled local agitators'. In South Uist too the land question 'is fast becoming an all-absorbing one here—the agitation seems spreading rapidly, and is taking shape in a very determined way'.

The progress of the agitation in Skye now suggested that 'in all probability the land agitation in this island will soon reach its climax. In the two most disaffected districts matters are surely coming to a crisis'. In Glendale, some of the men interdicted two years previously once again took over parts of the landlord's land. The crofters from one township in the district seized the farm of Scor. They destroyed the fences to gain access for their cattle, and when the landlord's nephew and a shepherd went to drive away the cattle, a great crowd of crofters was summoned by the horns of their watchmen, and Dr Martin's nephew was warned away, and told not to interfere again with the new stock on his uncle's field. All crofters had been advised by the local League to put their stock on the occupied land, and those who, like one of Martin's former shepherds, did not, were subjected to the persuasive attentions of a League delegation. Pressure was also brought to bear on any who did not attend meetings of the League: the miller of Kilmuir, who had failed to attend a League meeting at Quiraing, found his corn-stacks scattered to the wind. Similar instances of land-seizure, and similar tactics to ensure solidarity, were occuring throughout the Western Isles.

By the end of October, the sixty strong Glenelg branch of the League was 'prospering greatly', and meeting weekly in the MacBrayne's storehouse there under the chairmanship of mason Donald Macleod. The people of

Barra were 'extremely interested in land reform— wherever two or three are gathered together, one may safely wager that the land is the subject of conversation'. At the beginning of November, the new style of agitation was still on the increase in Skye. Deeds of lawlessness, such as seizing proprietors' lands, placing stock there, intimidating shepherds from interfering with such stock, scattering the corn-stacks and burning the peat stacks of crofters who did not join, and 'assaults upon such, are becoming altogether too frequent to be put up with much longer'. In Glendale, crofters had placed stock on the farms of Waterstein and Scor, and proposed ploughing old arable lands in the proprietors' hands; all of them were to sow a given quantity of seed there in the spring, and the produce would be shared between them in the autumn. 'Wilder schemes are discussed, and deeds that would shock the people some ten years ago are now coolly proposed'.

Meanwhile, in Lewis, four hundred crofters in Uig were more firmly than ever on rent-strike by November, and lands had been seized from the estate and the large farmers. On one occasion a farmer attempted to put his own stock on some of the occupied land; but a hundred men removed him and his stock with threats of violence should he persist with his attempt. In the parish of Lochs the people were also on rent-strike, and so well-organised was the agitation, that those who privately claimed a willingness to pay rent did not dare to do so, for fear of instant retribution. By November 14th, all non-crofter grazing land in Uig had been occupied; in Lochs, no-rent proclamations had been issued from the townships of Crossbost, Ranish, Luerbost, Calbost, Marvig and Gravir. The people of Cromore had also re-possessed land, which they had seized from the sheep farmer, removing his stock and replacing it with their own. Between the townships of Gravir and the farm of Orinsay a boundary dyke had been built to keep the poor and their stock off the wealthy farmer's land; in the second week of November, bands of men destroyed it; and in Gravir itself, a Free Church elder and crofter was declared boycotted and outcast for having broken the strike and paid his rent.

Away in the south, in Edinburgh and in London, the Lord Advocate and his colleagues were becoming distinctly worried at what was happening in the Highlands. The landlords and wealthy tenant-farmers had been complaining bitterly at events in Lewis and Skye, and in the other islands too; the fear was widespread among them that their wealth and even their persons might fail to survive the agitation should it go unchecked much longer. From Lewis, Uist and Skye, there were reports of the circulation of an 'infamous handbill', addressed to all crofters. The document in question read: 'Stand up like men before your oppressors! Demand restoration of the rights of which you have been robbed! The enemy is the landlord ... burn the property of all obnoxious landlords ... set fire to the heather to destroy the game; disturb the deer; poison game dogs! The oppressed toilers and the millions of the disinherited people are watching your actions. Their hearts are with you in your battle for rights and liberty. God save the people!'

In short, matters had reached the stage where it seemed that Highland landowners might soon find themselves ejected in their turn from the land which they and their fathers had taken from the people. This was not a prospect they—or the authorities—relished; and it was consequently determined, as a last resort, to call in the Navy. This was a distinctly dangerous gamble, a last attempt to stabilise a situation which seemed otherwise to give notice of full-scale social conflict in the Highlands, with unimaginable implications for the rest of the country. As a venue for the final crushing of crofter sedition, the authorities chose the island of Skye.

Sheriff Ivory's marines

'We are frugal and not extravagant
in our way of living, our staple
food being meal, potatoes, fish when
it is got ... We have very miserable
dwelling-houses, and never got aid
from our proprietors to build better
ones. They are thatched with straw;
and as our crofts do not produce the
required amount of straw necessary for
fodder for the cattle and thatch for
our houses, and as we are prohibited from
cutting rushes or pulling heather by the
proprietor, the condition of our dwelling-houses
in rainy weather is most deplorable.
... Of the twenty crofters' houses, there
are only two in which the cattle are not under
the same roof with the family. Now we leave
it to your Lordship to see what this revelation
of the condition of our dwellings reflects on
the boasted civilisation of the ninteenth
century.'

JOHN MACPHERSON

For Superintendent Donald Aitchison, Deputy Chief Constable of Inverness-shire, and for Inspector Malcolm MacDonald of Portree, it had been a terrible day. It was eleven o'clock at night before they managed back to the safety of the Caledonian Hotel in Portree, exhausted, dispirited, and soaked to the skin. Even then, their work was not finished; Aitchison at once got the inspector to make the telegraph clerk open his office so that the Chief Constable himself, in the comfort of his villa in faraway Inverness, might know without delay of their endeavours. 'None of us injured,' Aitchison wired at midnight, 'but shoved and kicked all the way. We can't go back. Inspector thinks that the sooner we are off, the better, from the threats of the crowd. Wire orders'.

Chief Constable McHardy replied at once. 'Stay there', he ordered; 'consult the sheriff and the fiscal in Portree; report by post'. And as Aitchison and MacDonald laboriously prepared their reports, it became clear that neither had relished the previous day's work. For five hours they had stumbled in the dark hills. 'The day and night were very stormy, with rain and high winds. We were all wet to the skin,' wrote Aitchison. 'We are all quite tired and done up ... the inspector thinks the sooner the men are withdrawn the better ... quite done up and tired ... the inspector is not yet clear of the last outrage that was committed on him; his legs are still swelling. I was not myself feeling strong before coming here, but I hope that the weakness I feel will pass away'. The inspector too had many complaints. They had kept on under a drenching rain, he wrote, until they came within four miles of Portree, where they had been met by Mr Murdo Gillanders, Depute Procurator Fiscal, with two conveyances he had taken from Portree to meet them—and just in time, for the superintendent and he were giving up with fatigue, from the ill-treatment they had received from the crowd. He was very much bruised, 'and it is with difficulty I can move about with the pain in my legs. They are swollen from my ankles to my thighs. I got two severe blows on the back, which is still painful. I observed as we were driven along by the crowd, several sticks raised above the superintendent's head, with threats to smash his head'.

In the morning the Chief Constable wired again, hoping that his deputy and his men were all feeling better and in comfortable quarters; and instructing them to remain in Skye until further orders. To McHardy, the discomfort of his men represented a golden opportunity; for whereas Aitchison and MacDonald both wanted a withdrawal from Skye, McHardy on the other hand saw the prospect of a spectacular end to his years of successful service as a police-officer. After all, he was Chief Constable of a county in which, in the landward areas at least, crime was all but unknown, a county whose population was, in terms of conventional criminal offences, remarkably law-abiding. To a man nearing the end of his career, the prospect of national fame beckoned alluringly and irresistibly. Should Skye become a matter of national attention, then so too would Skye's Chief Constable—and what man could resist the lure of urgent correspondence with the Home Secretary, the Lord Advocate, important business visits to London, mentions in the newspapers, the Houses of Parliament, maybe even the Cabinet itself? And what further honour or advancement might not await a man of such proven wisdom and experience and such important acquaintance, when he shortly relinquished his present post?

The prospects were indeed attractive; moreover, events in Skye in previous months had given McHardy cause for real concern. In June he had reported on matters there to a special sub-committee of the County Police Committee, and by the end of October, he had to report that the state of land agitation in the island was even more serious than earlier in the year. The facts which caused him such disquiet, and which led up to his men's discomfiture, were as follows. In early June, John Campbell of Hamara in Glendale, the son of a crofter, had driven his father's cattle onto the landlord's grazing-land; when the landlord's cattleman drove off Campbell's nine stirks, he simply returned them again. Then, in mid-June, Campbell's stirks were again removed, and again replaced instantly on the Hamara land. Next, Campbell was offered temporary use of grazing-land at Ramasaig. When the landlord instructed him to move from there at the end of August, he refused; and, going instead to the Uist cattle market, brought more cattle home to Skye with which to increase his stock on the forbidden ground. Elsewhere in the district, crofters had meanwhile taken possession of Dr Martin's land. In September, Neil MacPherson of Milovaig had his cattle on the proprietor's farm of Waterstein, in defiance of the interdict of 1882; and it was in the same month that the lands of Scor were appropriated by the crofters.

By October, all the crofters of Upper and Lower Milovaig were grazing their stock on the farm at Waterstein. In Glendale, therefore, the summer and autumn of 1884 witnessed a quiet and steady process of land-expropriation by the landless and the land-hungry—a gradual and unspectacular process, which nevertheless would eventually have forced the most determined reaction from the proprietors. But by the end of October, as McHardy stated in his second report to the special police sub-committee, there were even more alarming indications of dis-affection and sedition. He drew the sub-committee's attention to the deliberate destruction of the proprietor's stock-fence at Waterstein, where half a mile of fence had been broken, the winders destroyed and the straining posts smashed with a heavy boulder. Even more alarming were reports and rumours of the formation of secret anti-landlord societies; as he put it to Lord Lovat and Sheriff Ivory, secret societies existed in the district for the purpose of committing outrages on proprietors and their property, and also for the injury of persons unfavourable to the crofters' agitation.

In Kilmuir, the summer of 1884 was marked by the same developments as occurred in Glendale; in this district, the Chief Constable reported in October, matters had now come to crisis at Uig. In one township, the whole crofting population had resisted the efforts of Major Fraser's manager to remove their stock from the major's grazing-land. 'Meetings of the local branch of the Land League have been frequently held throughout the district, and large gatherings of the people have taken place at the Kilt Rock, Quiraing ... each crofter agreed to pay ten shillings, and each cottar five shillings, agreeing not to do any work to any of the district farmers, and that under pain of injury to person or property ... They have appointed persons to watch over the district to see that these directions are carried out'.

It was in Kilmuir that matters finally came to a head. When Lord Napier and his Commissioners had visited Kilmuir, the evidence of the crofters had been bitterly critical of the proprietor's management of the estate. Shortly afterwards, the local policeman was exposed by Alexander Mackenzie for attempting to get the Kilmuir crofters to sign, under false pretences, a document retracting the criticisms they had voiced before Lord Napier. Mackenzie reported the sergeant to McHardy, who summoned him to the police headquarters in Inverness; but before he could be transferred elsewhere, he had been given a new job—as ground officer to Major Fraser back in Kilmuir. It was thus hardly surprising that, as the Home Secretary later informed the House of Commons, there was a 'special animosity' against the police in Kilmuir. And McHardy's alarm at this animosity was only increased by reports reaching him throughout October of the growing strength and confidence of the League there. Back in September he had applied to the Home Office for a supply of revolvers with which to arm his men in Skye; in response to his request, the War Office sent him fifty pistols, and twenty rounds of ammunition for each. In October however, he was telling the special sub-committee, 'respectfully but candidly', that the available force of police under his command was entirely inadequate to maintain order, and carry out the law. The reports from Kilmuir were now becoming even more alarming; for he understood that the crofters of Kilmuir had now decided to summon three local farmers to appear before their next mass-meeting, with the threat of force if they refused, to explain anti-crofter sentiments they had expressed before the Napier Commission. This last item was reported in the House of Commons, on the basis of McHardy's report, by the Home Secretary. Alexander Mackenzie wrote to Harcourt denouncing this report as a mere fabrication, an excuse for the self-aggrandisement of the Inverness authorities and landlords; and two of the three men allegedly summoned to appear before the crofters wrote to the *Inverness Courier* publicly denying all knowledge of such summonses. But to Major Fraser, and to McHardy, this opportunity to punish the impudence of the tenantry was too good to miss. 'In anticipation of these outrages' (as McHardy put it), Major Fraser demanded extra police, as a protection for his three friends. On Thursday, 23rd October, Major Fraser intimated that he had now received such alarming accounts from Uig, that he was 'under the necessity of applying for some additional police to be concentrated at Portree or Uig, so as to be prepared for any outbreak, the risk of which their presence might help to avert'. The following Tuesday, a committee consisting of McHardy, Lord

Lovat, the procurator-fiscal and the police committee clerk acceded to Major Fraser's application; and the very next morning six men were sent to Skye under the Deputy Chief Constable, with instructions to double the number of constables at each station in the district of Uig and Kilmuir, 'to preserve the peace, prevent crime or outrage, and to maintain the law forcibly if need be'.

All day Aitchison and his men travelled west, by train to Strome Ferry and thence by steamer and it was not until evening that Braes and Ben Lee slid past to port, and they sailed into the bay at Portree, where they were met by Inspector MacDonald of the local Constabulary Office. Less than two days remained before the proposed mass meeting at Quiraing, before which the three anti-crofter farmers were allegedly to be taken.

At three o'clock the following afternoon Aitchison's reinforcements set out for Uig—the superintendent himself, the inspector, a sergeant from Dunvegan, a sergeant from Beauly, and five constables from Skye and Inverness. They had hoped to leave earlier in the day, but could find no one willing to hire them the necessary carts, and it required the persuasion of Sheriff Speirs before these could be acquired from the local hotels. Even then, they got permission to take them only as far as Glenhinisdale Bridge, nearly five miles short of Uig; and while these negotiations were taking place, their departure was anticipated by the despatch of a telegram to Uig with warning that the police were coming, and instructions that they should be turned back. Macinnes of the Portree Hotel was a keen ally of the crofters, and also a close friend of the Portree postmaster, so the procurator-fiscal informed Aitchison; despite his suspicions, however, he could prove nothing against either of them. Thus the Uig people were making their preparations to meet the police even before they left Portree, and Aitchison could only report back from Portree that 'the postmasters here and at Uig are greatly in favour of the crofters'. Within a few hours of leaving the town that Thursday afternoon, he was to discover just how inconvenient such collaboration was for police operations in the Isle of Skye.

When the party arrived at Glenhinisdale Bridge, the boundary between Lord MacDonald's property and the Kilmuir estate, they found nothing but mist, and blinding rain obscuring the hills. They drove on for another two miles, and were then abandoned by the drivers, who lashed their horses back into the mist towards Portree. The nine of them walked on alone, nervous and dispirited, their regulation capes and helmets streaming in the steady downpour, the Skye men doubtful in their loyalties and the East Coast men doubtful in their resolve. For an hour they walked, in the incessant rain and the gathering dark of a dirty autumn night, until, within two hundred yards of their quarters in Uig Inn, they were halted as a band of crofters, hundreds strong, materialised from the mist, on the road itself, on their left and on their right. James Urquhart, a farmer and the keeper of the Uig Inn, was one of those who was to be arraigned before the Quiraing meeting on the morrow; among the men now barring the path of the superintendent and his party stood Urquhart's own coachman, Martin Martin of Uig, along with the assembled strength of the members and supporters of the land movement in the parish of Kilmuir. Urquhart himself had already been warned that the people had resolved not to tolerate him granting accommodation to the forces of proprietorial law and order; and the people were ready now to make good that resolve, by force if necessary.

'They appeared to be waiting for us', Inspector MacDonald wrote later; when they saw the police, 'they gave a yell that sounded something fearful in the glen, and marched to meet us, yelling and cheering, shouting and whistling, as they were approaching us'. Aitchison resolutely led his men towards them, until the party was compelled to halt, face to face with the unmoving crofters. 'They kept up a ringing cheer,' said MacDonald, 'and yelling for about three minutes, after we stood there, asking us very wildly, and with fierce oaths, where we were going, what took us here, who sent us here, and what were our reasons for coming here'. The superintendent informed the crowd that he had come among them so that the law might be preserved in Kilmuir; the people howled and yelled and cheered, and jeered that his services were not needed, and that what Kilmuir lacked was not law, but justice to the people. Aitchison was informed that he and his men must leave and that they had better go at once, for another three hundred and fifty men were on their way over the hills; and, as he put it in his report back to Inverness, 'they thereupon came upon us in a rush and said that they were seeing us so few, that it was not worth their while to handle us roughly, and then they forced us back'. For four and a half miles they were driven thus, being pushed, shoved, and hurried on back to Portree. The inspector heard orders given in the crowd for messengers to run towards Earlish, the township they were now approaching, 'to call out the people there to help them in driving away the dogs, as they called us, and such messengers ran on before us.' And when they were passing Earlish, the inspector saw an number of the people from there joining the crowd, each armed with a stick; and then their threats became fearful, 'wanting to strip us all of our clothing and shoes, and to drive us naked and barefooted along the road to Portree'. All the time, Aitchison recalled, the crofters were threatening him most fearfully, and were cursing and swearing at him in a frightful manner. They were also cheering and hooting at the pitch of their voices, and saying that should Major Fraser be there, 'he would be driven back along with us. They were highly excited. They said that they would resist five thousand policemen, and that should that number come they might bring their coffins with them'.

At Glenhinisdale Bridge, in the dark and the pouring rain, the procession halted, a silent and ominous ring of crofters around the nine policemen. Why were they there, someone asked. To reinforce the Uig police force, Constable MacLaren. Who had sent them? The Chief Constable of the county. Did they have summonses for anyone? No, they did not. Would they promise not to return? No, Aitchison could not so promise. It was eloquent testimony to the discipline of the Kilmuir people—two hundred angry and determined crofters surrounding nine bedraggled policemen in the autumn dark—that Aitchison's courageous response provoked no violence. Questions, indeed, had been accompanied by the persuasive suggestion that should they not be answered, the police might find themselves driven over the twenty foot high bridge. As it was, the crofters' spokesmen assured the police that they should be thankful that no blood had been drawn; and the Deputy Chief Constable of Inverness-shire assured them, civilly enough, that they were indeed grateful.

For a long moment, there was silence; then the ring broke, the people moved back, and the police were driven over the estate boundary; 'with one ringing cheer, they saw us past the bridge'. Passing Kensaleyre, the party heard a warning horn sound in the darkness; men suddenly appeared and briefly followed them, then hooted in derision, and again disappeared in the night; for another hour they trudged on until, within an hour's march of Portree, the depute procurator came upon them with two carts, and carried them home.

For the police, it had been an ignominious rout; and, most galling of all, it had been a rout not at the hands of a lawless rabble, but at the hands of a disciplined and determined body of men whose society was so structured that anti-social crime was almost entirely unknown to it. In fact, they had taken their own policemen, Constable MacLaren, to Uig with them to meet Aitchison that day, and he had remained in their ranks throughout the pursuit to Glenhinisdale Bridge. As Aitchison reported to Inverness: 'The crowd asked what brought us there. I told them and so also did Inspector MacDonald, that we were sent there to keep the peace. They replied that they never broke the peace ... that their own policeman was there, and that he was a good man and no more required. They thereupon asked Constable MacLaren whether they ever did anything, and he answered that they did not'. And MacDonald, describing the episode at Glenhinisdale Bridge, stated that 'when the crowd formed the ring, I saw PC MacLaren with them ... Some in the crowd pointed to him, saying, "That's our policeman, we brought him here with us tonight, we will bring him safe back, and take care of him"'.

In the days following, as MacLaren cautiously reported to Portree, the people of Kilmuir made ready and organised themselves to face a major police assault upon their community. Meanwhile, the police faced difficulties over accommodation, transport, communications, and intelligence. They were watched unobtrusively but closely, and any signs of movement on their part were promptly signalled ahead. The people of Portree were distinctly unsympathetic to the police, wishing them gone from the island, even though it was in the west of the island that further police activity was most actively anticipated. Rumours of massive police reinforcements swept round the island. In Kilmuir, Aitchison reported, the people were quite ready and determined to resist any body of police, 'should they be 300 strong'. In the middle of the Sunday night following the confrontation, a clerk in Lord MacDonald's office in Portree reported that there were hundreds of people massed and waiting at Glenhinisdale Bridge, with clubs and weapons, waiting for the police. All the previous day a small party had watched over the road to Uig, to turn the procurator-fiscal back, should he attempt to go there. That same night, Dr Matheson was awakened at midnight from his bed in the Uig Inn, by sounds similar to the whistle of a steamer; thinking there was a steamer in the bay, he went to his bedroom window, 'and then saw the people on the road, and coming along the road; ... there were hundreds of them, the road being covered with them for a long distance, and they were armed with sticks'. A party had been sent to watch from the top of the highest rock in the district, too, to sound a timely alarm if any steamer should approach the bay at Uig. And as Monday wore on, the rumour grew and flew throughout Kilmuir that 150 police were on their way; all night long a watch was kept for them, and a party was in readiness to receive them should they come.

All that week the people remained in readiness. Aitchison was by now back in the safety of Inverness, but maintained close contact with Inspector MacDonald in Portree. On Thursday the inspector tele-grammed: 'Great excitement prevailing in Uig and Eastside today; watchers on all conspicuous places, armed with long sticks, short ones done away with; were told that a large force were going. Ready to resist any force'. On the Friday he wired again, to report 'great excitement today. Crowds going about Uig'. The next day Constable McLaren reported from Uig to Portree: 'Great excitement prevailing in district. Still determined to resist any police force whatsoever ... Groups constantly on watch. Police expected during Sunday'. And on the following Monday the inspector wired that the people were as prepared as ever: 'People going about in great numbers about one in the morning', he wired, 'waiting for receiving police; great meeting held at top of Rha yesterday evening, watchmen posted all over Kilmuir ... Whatever number of police may go they would require to be well protected ... the crofters are so determined that they would sooner die than yield to the police. The agitation throughout the whole island is in the highest degree, and undoubtedly all would turn out'.

The stage was thus set for an initiative which (it was thought in official circles) would finally crush the movement. In a memorandum to the Government, written that same weekend, McHardy explained why the sedition of the Kilmuir tenantry must not go unchecked any longer. Since the previous Thursday, he wrote, the people of Kilmuir had mobilised and held possession of the district, determined to debar the police from entering or going among them. They had for the past week been assembled in hundreds, day and night, and armed with sticks for the purpose of assaulting an expected body of police. A reign of terror existed in the district, 'and nothing short of government aid or protection for the police in restoring order and maintaining the law will suffice'.

McHardy's solution, which was favoured also by Sheriff Ivory and the

Lord Advocate, was to send the military to Skye; and that week their plan was to come to fruition, and to gain for McHardy and Ivory the national fame to which they both so obviously aspired. Their campaign to pressurise the Government into sending a gunboat and a force of marines was well planned. The very day after Aitchison's party had been expelled from Kilmuir, Lord Lovat chaired a meeting of the special police sub-committee, of which Ivory was also a member.

The committee resolved to press for the despatch of more men to Skye, for night patrols in the disaffected districts, and for any reinforcements to be armed and openly instructed in the use of firearms at Portree. It also suggested that such reinforcements be mounted, and that 'an application should be made to Government to station a gunboat with marines at Portree ... with such a number of marines as will be sufficient, not only to protect the police constables in the performance of their duty in preserving the peace, but to quell any riots with which the constables may be found unable to contend'. The clerk of the committee was instructed to 'crave of the Government the favour of an early compliance with the request for the services of a warship'; and he wrote the same night to the Home Secretary to that effect.

On Sunday, 2nd October, Sheriff Ivory wrote to the Lord Advocate, claiming to be 'of opinion that the immediate despatch of a gunboat and marines to Skye is absolutely necessary to protect the police and assist them in protecting the property and persons of the lieges in that island'. The Chief Constable had already assured Ivory that he was completing arrangements for sending as many additional men to Skye as possible, and hoped to have at least forty or fifty there by Wednesday next, all of whom would be armed with revolvers. On Tuesday, 4th October, McHardy heard from shippers David MacBrayne of Glasgow that they would be pleased to charter him the steamship *Lochiel,* at a rate of £200 per week, with meals at four shillings for officers and three shillings for other ranks. The reason for this expedient was, the Chief Constable explained, that 'as no accommodation can be got for the police nor means of conveyance through the island, the police authority have chartered a steamer for that purpose'. Next day McHardy wrote to Home Secretary Harcourt assuring him that, by the following Tuesday, fifty men, the whole available force at his command, would be concentrated at Portree. By now, Harcourt had already told the House of Commons that the conduct of the Skye crofters could no longer be tolerated, and that it was 'the duty of the local authorities, with the entire support of the Executive Government, to take all such measures as may be necessary to the observance of the law'.

By the second weekend in November, the *Lochiel* was waiting at Stornoway, ready to steam south to Strome to collect the force of police early in the coming week. McHardy and Ivory were in London, conferring with the Home Office; and Lord Archibald Campbell spent the weekend frantically telegramming to Skye, urging its crofters to succumb to lawful authority and insisting that only a return to the passivity of former years would yield an answer to their grievances. But the time for such lordly and gratuitous advice was long past, and his admonitions had no effect. A mass meeting had been planned at Kilmuir, at which as many as two thousand men were expected, from all parts of Skye, to resist the now well-publicised military threat. A violent gale which blew on the Friday and Saturday made the mass meeting impossible to hold; on the latter day some of the Kilmuir men were in Portree, where they heard the news that no troops were likely to appear in Skye until Monday or Tuesday. They returned to Kilmuir with this information; and that night at midnight, 'out of a pious regard for the sanctity of the Lord's Day, all the sentries on duty throughout the district were withdrawn and a suspension of hostilities for twenty-four hours was proclaimed'.

On the Monday a further report from Inverness indicated that the police reinforcements had still not left, as Ivory and the Chief Constable had yet to return from London; and a message from Stornoway let the Skyemen know that the *Lochiel* was still there, and that her captain and crew 'had positively refused to serve in the ungrateful task in carrying armed men for the purpose of shooting down their helpless and undefended brethren' on Skye. On Tuesday, Land League members in Stornoway telegrammed: '*Lochiel* crew refuse to proceed to Skye; thousands of Lewismen threatening to proceed to Skye to help crofters. Great excitement here'. Then the news flew round Kilmuir that the gunboat *Forester* had steam up and was under orders for Skye, under Captain Hodgkinson; next morning she was sighted by the Highland crew of the *Claymore* in the Sound of Mull; she called briefly at Tobermory, rounded Ardnamurchan Point within the hour, and the Cuillins of Skye stood out clear before her.

By Wednesday the *Lochiel* was coaling at Stornoway for extended service, her owners' agent telegramming south in an attempt to secure a crew for her. McHardy arrived back in Inverness from London, having concluded his consultations with the Home Secretary. His men were already assembled and ready to move to Skye. The *Assistance* and the gunboat *Banterer* were on their way north to join the *Forester*. At four o'clock in the afternoon, 'with a great calm over the land and sea', the *Forester* herself hove into Portree Bay and her anchors went down within half a mile of the shore. Her four guns, with an officer and eight men for each, and an extra six transferred from the *Shannon*, represented the first stage of the Government's attempt to return Skye to order, law, and impartial justice.

The next morning the *Lochiel* arrived at Strome, where she was met by her new skipper and special crew, 'in room of Captain Cameron and the Highland crew who have refused duty'; and on Saturday afternoon she too arrived in the bay at Portree, with twenty-five police, Ivory, McHardy, and the Inverness fiscal, who had all travelled down on the nine o'clock train that morning. On Sunday morning the *Assistance* arrived, with 350 marines and a hundred bluejackets; the next afternoon the *Banterer* arrived at Portree, with sixty-five more marines.

Sheriff Ivory, the Procurator-Fiscal and Chief Constable McHardy on the Lochiel, entering Portree Bay. They had come to Skye, to supervise its invasion by the force of marines ordered there to quell the land agitation.

Marines land on Major Fraser's Kilmuir estate; 'the district was found in a state of the most perfect peace...'

111

'The long-threatened expedition to the country of the crofters is now an accomplished fact..'; marines march into the Kilmuir estate.

By then the other three had sailed for Uig. The *Forester,* the slowest of them, had left at dawn; passing Staffin the *Assistance* had taken the lead, and she was the first to steam into the bay at Uig, anchoring off about four cables. The *Lochiel* came in, swept round the bay, and anchored to the south; while the *Forester* steamed in at noon, and dropped her anchors off the village, in position to cover with her guns the small-boats landing the marines. In the afternoon seven police came ashore, and with them came Ivory, McHardy, Aitchison, the fiscal, the Captain of the *Assistance,* and the Lieutenant-Colonel commanding her marines. They proceeded to the hotel, where they were refused accommodation; the police were sent to the school and the dignitaries returned by steam-launch to their ships. Then, as darkness fell seventy marines came ashore, in full marching order, detailed to guard the police and save them from the depradations of the Kilmuir tenantry.

It was an impressive demonstration of power, against an unarmed and impoverished population. Yet the crofters of Skye had their own answer to military might. Like every successful movement of agrarian peoples before or since, they recognised the hopelessness of attempting to resist a powerful military force; and the vigilante bands, lately so much in evidence, disappeared as if they had never existed. Instead, the crofters donned the garb of passive resistance—a tactic founded on the precept that no power can subjugate a whole people unless they accept the authority of that power. The people were not to disobey the direct orders of the forces of law and order; but neither would they do those things which were a necessary prelude to the restoration of the authority of the landlords. The principles they were to observe had been minutely explained and passionately expounded, by the leaders of the League and by local spokesmen, and at meetings of the people themselves. It was agreed that they would not attack police or marines—but neither would they pay rent, withdraw from occupied fields, or accept the arrest of any interdicted or

112

summonsed crofter except on a token basis. John MacPherson told Ivory all this when he met him aboard ship at Portree; and the strongly pro-League Rev Davidson of Stenscholl, himself one of those under notice from Major Fraser to quit his croft in Kilmuir, re-affirmed them when he met Ivory in Uig.

The principle was simple, the decision to use it masterful; given the support and participation of the mass of the population, passive resistance was a tactic no gunboat could begin to combat. As the ships steamed round to Uig, there was no demonstration anywhere on the coast; at every township along the coast the people were ostentatiously and conspicuously at work, digging potatoes. At Staffin, where opposition had been expected, 'the utmost quietude and decorum prevailed'; and when the flotilla steamed into Uig itself, 'the crofter population made big efforts to look busy. Not a single crofter came down to the shore, either to defy or welcome the huge troopship'. As the special correspondent of the *Glasgow Herald* observed, somewhat sadly, 'The long threatened expedition to the country of the crofters is now an accomplished fact ... The district was found in a state of the most perfect peace, with every crofter minding his own business ... A descent today was made upon Uig, and with results which must be described so far as entirely unsatisfactory'.

Ivory, however, was not beaten yet. At nine o'clock the next morning, 250 armed marines were disembarked at the head of Uig Bay, in preparation for a pacificatory march on Staffin, nine miles away. Resplendent in red and white, their arrival on the beach was announced to the people of Uig by a party of buglers. Preceded by twenty marine artillery, and by Ivory, McHardy, and the other officials, the expedition set off in marching order to bring peace to Kilmuir. The marine commander rode on a pony, commandeered from the Inn; from this vantage he surveyed his little army of advance guards, officials, marines, and police. As scouting parties moved ahead, he saw the *Forester* and the *Lochiel* steam north to rendezvous at Staffin, and disappear from sight beyond the bay. Soon it began to rain, and by the time they reached Staffin, four hours later, it was raining heavily, so that the *Forester* and the *Lochiel,* now joined from Portree by the *Banterer,* could scarcely be seen in the bleak, grim bay. Ivory and his officials, along with the officers, took refreshments at the Lodge; fifty marines were left there; and the flotilla steamed back to Uig, leaving the *Banterer* to impress Staffin. Night fell, 'amid a scene of perfect tranquility on the part of the villagers'.

The weather worsened; all Wednesday and Thursday, a strong northerly gale kept the fleet at anchor in Uig, and Ivory's intention to storm Glendale by sea was frustrated. By Friday morning, however, the weather had improved, and within two hours, the *Assistance,* the *Forester* and the *Lochiel* were at anchor off Dunvegan. The sheriff, the Chief Constable, the fiscal and the Lieutenant-Colonel led ashore twenty police and three companies of marines, and set out to march to Hamara Lodge, Glendale. On the hillcrest the party came upon a meeting of six hundred members of the League, just as Free Church elder John Mackay was closing it with a Gaelic prayer. The marine buglers provocatively attempted to disrupt the proceedings; but the provocation was ignored, and the meeting dispersed with dignity and discipline, leaving Ivory to station at Hamara six police, seventy-five marines, a week's rations, and 3,000 rounds of amunition.

At the very moment when the Land Leaguers of Glendale were quietly dispersing, the Duke of Argyll was explaining to his fellow peers in the House of Lords what the agitation in the Highlands was all about. It had nothing to do with any grievances of the crofters (who had none), but was merely an ignorant attempt to obstruct the interests of progress in the Highlands. According to the Duke, events in Skye and elsewhere were to be termed the work of an 'active propoganda of social agitation'. The lawlessness which had compelled the Government to send an armed force to Skye had been serious, and he wished to describe the length to which it had gone. It was not a question of resisting rent as being too high; it was not a question of resisting evictions or removals; 'it is a question of seizing other people's lands. They have entered on the land and seized it by main force and I will only say that if such a state of things is allowed to go on, all capital will be driven from the country'. And as the Duke sat down, having drawn attention to the disgrace of landless crofters taking land from those with plenty of it, the Lords, mindful of the horrors of popular land-ownership, assented rapturously.

It was, indeed, to prevent such expropriations from becoming general that the gunboats had been sent to the north; and, as Sheriff Ivory himself knew, the protection of landed property, which motivated his expedition to Skye, meant continued poverty and land-hunger for thousands of crofters. The Government, by backing the landlords at this juncture, had given new substance to the notion of a class war in the Highlands, All Saturday the fleet lay off Dunvegan; then, on Sunday at dawn, twenty-five marines and constables were landed there with supplies for a fortnight. The *Forester* stayed to back them up, while the *Assistance* and the *Lochiel* sailed at noon for Portree, there to await instructions from the Lord Advocate himself. Ivory had already reported to him, and was keen to commence pacification of other areas and islands troubled with the effects of land-hunger and poverty; and on Monday coaling and provisioning was completed for Ivory's proposed assault on North Uist; but that evening, Harcourt intervened to prohibit such an expedition, 'for the time being'. His intervention marked a turning-point.

Next day, six hundred men from Valtos and Staffin unanimously agreed to pay no more rent to the Kilmuir proprietor; Ronald Maclean told them, 'We are now met under the most favourable circumstances in which we have yet stood. Go on then. Some would like you to be quiet now. Your fathers kept quiet—quiet ever since the '45. Tell me what they gained by it? Still keep up your agitation; let your enemies see you are not afraid of police or military—your agitation must and will go on until your wrongs are righted'.

Four of the police reinforcements stationed at Staffin had turned up at that meeting, but had been promptly expelled from it—a matter of some annoyance to Ivory, who found them, when he visited his garrison the next day at lunchtime, 'labouring under a sense of humiliation from the indignity heaped upon them at yesterday's meeting of crofters'. Otherwise, Ivory found little to report; his garrisons had simply been ignored by the crofters, who treated them as if their existence bore no relation whatsoever to anything connected with Skye or its crofting population. Not that the people of Skye were unfamiliar with the armed forces; as John Macleod of Earlish told 150 Land Leaguers at Uig on Thursday, Skye had in forty years furnished Her Majesty's forces with twenty-one lieutenant-generals, forty-five lieutenant-colonels, six hundred officers and ten thousand foot-soldiers. That meeting was held in a gale of wind and rain, high on the side of the nearest hill, 'in order that the Sheriff and armed men might see what was going on, and learn the fact that the men of Uig have not yet been frightened into forgetting their grievances'.

That afternoon, in Portree Sheriff Court, interdicts were granted against crofters in Stenscholl, Glendale and Dunvegan for land-seizure—but by the evening, the crofters had anticipated the order of the court, and removed their stock from the fields in question. Major Fraser, however, was determined to provoke a situation in which conflict was likely, in which the crofters might at last be outmanoeuvred, and give the marines and police an opportunity to use their bayonets and batons. It had not escaped him that, of the eighteen offenders at Stenscholl, one was the Rev Davidson and another was local branch secretary of the League.

The writs were served in the first week of November and there was no violence of any kind. Major Fraser's offer of a rent-reduction was refused. In Glendale, on the first day of the month, the tenants of the Glendale and Husabost estates had agreed that they would no longer pay any rent whatsoever; and on the following morning, when the Glendale factor called for his rents, not one crofter was there to pay him. The tenants of Fasach, indeed, wrote an explanatory letter to their landlord, in which they stated that they would pay no more rent, since they were not morally bound to do so. 'Our poverty is not our fault. We have worked ... to pay you for what should be our houses; but we are now so poor that we must first obey the law of nature, to feed and clothe ourselves, and we therefore cannot pay you any rent which you wish to exact from us'. On the way they had been deprived of land, they had this to say: 'Though it may have enriched you, it has impoverished us ... now, owing to thus being deprived, we consider that you are owing us £40, and, in all seriousness, we say that you should pay us this instead of asking us for rent. This would be but little return for the years of labour and adversity through which we have passed'.

In the weeks that followed, the incidence of rent-strikes showed a spectacular rise, with a fine disregard for the military presence and the punitive authority of the law courts. This was merely another tactic at the disposal of a movement which was not going to be thwarted by police or marines or landed family fortune. As John MacPherson told a meeting at Braes that week, at which it was made clear no more rent would be paid for Ben Lee, 'it would be as easy to stop the Atlantic Ocean as to stop the present agitation until justice has been done to the people.'

So the rent-strike spread, like a flooding tide, through Lord MacDonald's other lands in Skye. The estate had for many years been bled to subsidise the owners' expensive tastes; and even when his Lordship became confined in an Edinburgh mental institution, Lady MacDonald continued to entertain lavishly. At the great functions in Armadale Castle, the catering was superintended from Edinburgh. She herself would think nothing of disposing of 100 guineas on some trifling sartorial confection. For years she insisted on having on her luncheon table each day the tongue of an ox torn that morning from the mouth of that day's slaughtered carcase. For generations, the MacDonald's tenantry had borne the cost of that expenditure. By the end of the first week in November, 1884, however, the Braes strikers were joined by the tenants of many townships in Snizort. Duncan Macrae of Carbost told a meeting that it was MacDonald who was in debt to his tenants, rather than the tenants to MacDonald; those present agreed there and then to pay no more rent, pending redress of their grievances. John MacPherson and the Rev MacCallum, who respectively opened the meeting and closed it, fully endorsed this action. On Saturday night, MacDonald's Braes and Sconser tenants extended the strike to include all rents payable by them to the proprietor; their decision brought the number of no-rent townships on MacDonald land to fourteen. At the weekend, a thousand Kilmuir tenants met at Uig, and agreed unanimously to reject the factor's invitation to send delegates to him to discuss rents. It also endorsed the suggestion of Archibald MacDonald, the local League secretary, that Major Fraser himself be invited to appear before a mass-meeting of crofters to explain any offer he might have to make; and that, if any such offer were forthcoming, the crofters should respond to it only after a week or two spent considering it. After much discussion, the chairman asked for a show of hands of those able to pay rent; 'no hands were raised, and in response to the chairman's request that those who were not able and willing to pay rent to raise their hands, every man raised his hand'.

By the middle of December the Skye landlords were faced with the reality of not receiving any rents at all. Lord MacDonald owned all of the land in the parishes of Sleat and Strath, and most of it in Portree and Snizort. In the Portree parish, the rent-strike in Braes meant a loss of £500, while in Sleat, townships worth £700 in rent were now refusing to pay. Major Fraser of Kilmuir faced the prospect of losing £3,000 annually in rent; his thirty crofting townships in Kilmuir paid him £2,000, while his ten townships in Snizort were worth £800 a year. Lord MacDonald's Snizort tenants owed him £550, but he was unlikely to get it. 'The no-rent movement is spreading with great rapidity', stated a report from Skye. 'The crofters on the Kilmuir and Glendale estates have unanimously resolved to pay no rent at present, and township after township on the MacDonald estates is following the same example ... Mr Robertson, Greshornish, was last week in Glendale for the purpose of receiving the rent now due ... He spent a day at Milovaig, and invited the people to confer with him and pay their rents, but none responded. After remaining a few days at Hamara, he returned home without accomplishing the object of his visit'. Nor, as time went on, were the crofters prepared to pay their road, school and poor rates, because, as they argued, they often did not have roads, they were not allowed to use the school for their own purposes, and they seldom saw any official from the Poor Board. The Board, controlled as it was by the landlords and their factors, could do nothing about the crofters' refusal: their officers were already refusing to enter Braes to sequester crofters' furniture in lieu of rates, since one of them had been turned back and warned never to return; which he now refused to do. As a reprisal, MacDonald's factor told the Portree parish minister that he would no longer receive his stipend until the crofters paid their rates; and as for threats made by the crofters, that was a matter for the courts to deal with.

But with the mass of the crofters on strike, there was little that the authorities could do. If they could not break the unity and resolve of the people, they could not hope to defeat the popular will. After all, they could not gaol every crofter on Skye; and even if they could, the only sure effect would be to cut off, even more finally, the landlords' income from rent. Moreover, the Government did not dare risk an outbreak of serious violence; a bloodbath in Skye might, not inconceivably, have horrendous results for the rest of the country. Accordingly, the Government forbade the use of marines in serving notices of legal action for rent-arrears and land-seizures; and the Lord Advocate announced that no action was to be taken against the Uig men for the repulse of Superintendent Aitchison's party; he added, though, that retribution would follow if there were continued trouble on the island. By the end of the year, there had been no trouble, in the sense that the authorities had chosen not to recognise it as such, and had not dared to initiate large-scale proceedings against the thousands of crofters who were, in one way or another, blatantly breaking the law, and announcing openly that they were doing so, and that they intended to continue to do so.

The military expedition to Skye had little effect on the crofters' agitation, apart from giving it excellent publicity outside the Highlands, and offering grounds for increased pro-crofter agitation in Parliament. While Sheriff Ivory marched his men around Skye, the crofters' parliamentary spokesmen executed a shrewdly-timed manoeuvre: as the rent-strike spread, they pressed for an emergency Act of Parliament to prevent the eviction of crofters for rent-arrears, 'until such time as legislation is passed meeting their grievances'. As for the marines, they could not be used to fulfil the declared purpose of sending them there. The people of Skye showed no antipathy whatever to them, and within weeks, fraternisation was not uncommon. The crew of the *Assistance* organised a charity concert at Portree; Captain St Clair assured his audience that, 'setting aside the question of why they were there', they would never forget the kindness they received from the people of Skye. The Portree Rifle Club challenged the *Assistance* team of marksmen to a shooting competition; the Skyemen, ironically enough, were the victors.

For Ivory and McHardy, it had been a galling defeat. Over-ruled by their superiors, out-manoeuvred by the crofters, widely scorned in public, and calmly ignored by the strikers and the local leaders, they left Skye in the middle of December. The *Lochiel* was returned to her normal duties; the numbers at each garrison were drastically reduced—and Ivory's invasion fleet gradually steamed south, leaving the island under no more than a token occupation. To the crofters' movement, its departure made no more difference than its arrival. The agitation continued, on an even greater scale than before; and as the winter drew in, the tactics that had defeated Ivory in Skye were extended ever more widely across the Highlands.

In no friendly spirit

*'If the Government do not look
to the matter, they may soon
find themselves face to face
with an insurrection of the
labouring population in the
Highlands'.*

MESSRS STUART, RULE & BURNS

Inveraray Castle—home of the Duke of Argyll.

The home of a tenant on the island of Coll, Argyll.

As the year 1884 drew to a close the agitation continued to intensify and spread. The Duke of Argyll wrote in alarm to the Prime Minister, 'There can be no doubt that a Land League ... have got hold of all the Hebridean islands, which are now divided among the counties of Argyll, Inverness and Ross. The population amounts to upwards of 60,000'. What was especially worrying to the Duke was the effect the agitation might have on the membership of the House of Commons, if even more crofter spokesmen got into Parliament. Those already there had, in his opinion, caused sufficient trouble as it was; and it was with a plan to prevent such a development that His Grace now wrote to the Prime Minister. The franchise had just been extended; under massive pressure, the Government had extended the right to vote in parliamentary elections to a much wider section of the population than ever before; and was also preparing to redistribute the boundaries and locations of constituencies, to reflect the whereabouts of the increased electorate. The Duke, however, saw these imminent changes, not as the fulfilment of an obligation to bring about more equitable parliamentary representation but as the means to a quite different end.

The Duke's proposal to Gladstone was simple. That very morning he had discussed the whole question with young Munro Ferguson of Novar, whom he termed one of the 'most creditable young men whom Scotland has yet sent to Parliament', and had found the young Member for Ross-shire firmly of the opinion that, unless the strongest areas of land-leaguing were demarcated and cordoned off from the other areas of the Highlands, the effect would be to expel from the Commons Novar and all the other landed proprietors who represented Highland constituencies, and to replace them with men favourable to the newly-franchised masses in those constituencies. Such an addition to the House, thought His Grace, 'embracing some five county members and co-operating with a certain number from the cities, would be a formidable addition to the Party of Disorder'. The displacement of men like Novar by men like Fraser-Mackintosh 'would be a damage to stability, decency, justice, and most of all, progress'. Young Novar was certain to be expelled from his seat; for as soon as they had the chance to vote, he would be 'swamped by the cottars and crofters of the Lewis', with all their 'wild notions'. The Duke and Novar, therefore, proposed to Gladstone a simple remedy: make the Hebrides a separate constituency, abandoned to the crofters, in order to give the aristocracy a better prospect of holding on to the mainland Highland parliamentary seats. Novar had calculated that 'unless the Islands are separated and erected into a constituency by themselves, about five seats will be lost'; lost, thought the Duke, to naught but sedition and outrage. 'The extraordinary ignorance of these poor people', he told Gladstone, 'is incredible'.

But if the Duke found the beliefs and actions of the people to be ignorant beyond belief, events occurred daily which could amply explain them. By the first week of January, 1885, £2,000 was needed at once to meet the relief

The Duke of Argyll, who wrote 'It was well-known to many, but it was somewhat difficult to prove, that professional agitators preceded the Commission and instructed the poorer classes what they were to say'.

of poverty in Uig and Kilmuir, 'which is of an exceptional character and may be expected to be at its worst at the beginning of February'. The following week, Henry George was touring Skye, urging the people 'to take what was justly theirs'; he was especially well-received in Broadford and Portree, whence he was due to proceed to Lewis at the end of the week. At the same time Mr Winans, a millionaire landlord from overseas, brought Scotland's best advocate to Dingwall, to pursue an action against a Kintail crofter and shoemaker, for allowing his pet lamb to graze on land used by Winans for the purposes of game shooting. The distress in Kilmuir did not dissuade Major Fraser from continuing similar legal action against his tenants, and especially against the Rev Davidson; indeed, he argued in public that 'if under Land League direction tenants, who until of late have paid their rents so well, will not now pay them at all, and if no processes are to be used against them, how can landlords so placed recover their rents, or defend their non-crofter farms from seizure? And then, further, in such cases, how can those whose incomes may be derivable from their estates pay their accounts if the crofters cannot be called upon to pay theirs?'.

Clearly, the rent-strike was becoming painful; and by the end of January, 1885, it was in full swing throughout the Hebrides. Already, the Sheriff of Ross had visited Lewis aboard HMS *Seahorse*, for the purpose of arresting crofters who had deforced a messenger-at-arms while he was attempting to serve interdicts from the Court of Session. Moreover, the roads in the west of Lewis were impassable to all but the most determined; for they had all been blocked with boulders and obstacles, to prevent the progress of any police or military expedition. And in Skye, in the last week of January, sheriff-officers were deforced in Valtos and Glendale, while serving summonses for arrears of rent. On the last weekend of the month, a rumour hastened round Skye that the *Lochiel* had been chartered again, and that arrests on a large scale might be expected at any time in the next few days, whenever Ivory and McHardy arrived from Inverness with their police reinforcements. In fact, Harcourt had written that same month to the Lord Advocate, instructing him to 'make it quite clear to the Police Committee that Her Majesty's Government regard the military force as acting in support of, and not in substitution for, the police'. But the Sheriff of Inverness was not so easily dissuaded from his campaign against crofter lawlessness: on the first Thursday of February Ivory took twenty-five police and 200 marines to Glendale, and there arrested six crofters on charges of rioting and deforcement.

These arrests took place exactly a month after the repulse of the messenger-at-arms from Inverness, who, after serving only five of their fourteen summonses and notices, had been driven from the glen— 'somewhat roughly'—and forced to destroy the remaining papers in their possession. The authorities had determined at once on retribution, but made their preparations with the utmost secrecy. The day before the arrests, the *Lochiel* steamed from Strome direct for Dunvegan, and the police rode overnight from Portree. Soon afterwards the *Assistance* arrived on the scene, and she and the *Lochiel* commenced landing their forces, marines and officials respectively, just before dawn. Within an hour the whole party reached the glen and commenced the pre-arranged house searches. A crowd of women and children, hundreds strong, jeered the police, but there was no violent resistance. John MacPherson himself was in Glendale, home briefly after a speaking tour; he remonstrated both with Ivory and with the marine commander, Lieutenant-Colonel Munro, and assured the prisoners, as they were taken away, that they need not worry, because they would be back home again.

The next day, the *Lochiel* and the *Assistance* landed Ivory's force at Valtos. 'Immediately on landing, operations for arrest were commenced, but after a whole day's search the officers of the law were only successful in apprehending two out of the eight against whom warrants had been issued. The other six had betaken themselves with a number of others to the surrounding hills ... The excitement throughout the islands is intense'. In Valtos, there had been a serious struggle with the police, requiring a hundred marines to fix their bayonets; and that night, when the *Assistance* and the *Lochiel* reached Portree, close on midnight, it was thought unsafe to venture ashore, for fear of provoking a similar, or greater, struggle. All evening, a sizeable crowd of villagers had been on the lookout for the ships, and even at midnight there were still many assembled on the terrace looking out over the harbour, expecting the immediate disembarkation of the Glendale prisoners. 'As a result of the excitement that prevailed, the bells of the churches were rung at intervals by several of the young men, horns were blown and bagpipes were played. The uproar was maintained until near daybreak'.

Until well after daybreak the *Lochiel* and the *Assistance* continued to lie off from Portree pier, with the *Forester*, now back in Skye, alongside them. The *Banterer* was on station up in the north west, in Loch Dunvegan; and at ten in the morning the *Seahorse* steamed in from Staffin. Fifty marines went ashore under the Lieutenant-Colonel, formed in defensive order on the quayside, and, as the *Lochiel* came alongside, protected her gangways from the jeering, howling crowd at their backs. Ivory and McHardy came onto the pier, and thirty police escorted the prisoners who 'appeared in excellent spirits', and were greeted by the crowd 'with ringing cheers, again and again repeated'. The police formed four deep with the prisoners in their centre, and set out towards the County Buildings. Behind them came the marines, each armed with rifle and bayonet, and 'their ball pouches supplied with ammunition'. As the party proceeded from the quay and through Portree, 'the crowd, which was all the time increasing, exhibited the most intense excitement, howling and yelling in a most furious manner ... The excitement in Portree on Saturday night continued most intense, and the policemen who patrolled the streets were hooted and hissed in the wildest manner'.

The day of the arrests in Valtos, the Lochcarron branch of the League met outdoors in the village. In a long speech, the local president impressed upon the meeting the propriety of using all means to banish despotism, advised the crofters to prepare for the forthcoming general election and on no account to vote for anyone who was a landowner, 'and denounced the tyranny of the upper classes and the authorities who had attempted to intimidate and crush the crofters'. A second speaker remarked pointedly at the absence of the clergy from the meeting; with a few honourable exceptions, he noted, this seemed to be an increasing tendency with the ministers. Yet the opposite should be the case; and he therefore suggested, 'in order to bring the clergy to a sense of their duty and responsibility in this matter', that the people might try the experiment of withholding that part of their contributions to church funds which went towards ministers' stipends. Next to speak was John Maclean, a fisherman from Lochcarron. His theme was the injustice of a system which allowed souls to be crowded into a mere hundred and fifty acres of land so poor and rocky that the manure had to be carried up to the miserable plots on the backs of the people. In order to remedy this 'deplorable state of affairs' Maclean proposed that the extensive deer forest of Achnashellach should at once be broken up and apportioned among the people of the district; in support of his contention he produced a Bible, from whose pages he read out the first three verses of the ninth chapter of Genesis:

And God blessed Noah and his sons, and said unto them, Be fruitful, and multiply, and replenish the earth. And the fear of you and the dread of you shall be upon every beast of the earth, and upon every fowl of the air, upon all that moveth upon the earth; and upon all the fish of the sea; into your hand are they delivered. Every moving thing that liveth shall be meat for you; even as the green herb have I given you all things'.

That, cried the fisherman to his two hundred listeners, was stronger than any deed or title or charter of right of ownership ever granted by any mere earthly power; and he went on to move the adoption of the branch committee's resolution on land law reform. It demanded the destruction of all sheep-farms and deer-forests and their just apportionment among the crofting population; judicial fixing of fair rents; security of tenure; statutory recognition of these demands; 'that the legislature shall recognise the right of the cultivator to the value of his own labour and improvements, and shall not permit those to be robbed by the landlords as they have notoriously been'; and that Parliament recognise the principle that men must be allowed to live on their own native land. Legislation must be introduced 'to establish the reign of justice in the Highlands and Islands where it has been so long absent'; and finally, since 'leases between landlords and tenants of crofts would be evidence of the power of the landlords to still oppress those who cultivate God's earth', the men of Lochcarron would henceforth be no party to them. The motion went to the vote; the two hundred crofters present accepted it unanimously; and copies of the resolution were despatched forthwith to Edinburgh and London, for the attentions of the Lord Advocate, the Home Secretary and the Prime Minister.

The first week of February witnessed similar demands from the Stornoway branch of the League. From the Dalglish estate in Ardnamurchan it was reported that 'fears are now entertained that troublesome times are impending'. The crofters of Tiree were demanding reductions in their rent. The League branch in the Duke of Argyll's estate in the Ross of Mull was reported active and of especial worry to the authorities, since it had decided to conduct its meetings in private, and allow entry to no one but accredited members. On Skye, the League announced that it would arrange for the defence of the men arrested in Glendale and Valtos. And in South Uist, that same week, the people were busy taking possession of the lands once held by their fathers: thirty men from Lochboisdale formally took possession of a nearby island on which to plant potatoes; and it was reported that similar actions could soon be expected all over the island. At the week's end the Lochcarron branch of the League met again, to hear the Rev MacCallum remind them that evictions were still being effected in quiet corners of the Highlands; he recalled in particular 'a very cruel case of eviction in Arisaig last summer'. MacCallum was followed by John MacPherson, who assured his listeners that, from the very first, he had 'discerned the over-ruling hand of Providence in the agitation, and now rejoiced at the dimensions and importance it had assumed'. The following day, the largest land agitation meeting ever held in Caithness was convened in Thurso Town Hall; the meeting demanded the destruction of deer-forests, the granting of more land to the crofters, and the implementation of the proposals of the Napier Commission.

In Daliburgh in South Uist, three fields were taken from the landlords for potato patches, and the remonstrations of the factor summarily rejected. In Lewis, four hundred men gathered at a 'very enthusiastic' meeting at the Free Church in Barvas; their demands were identical to those echoing across the Highlands. On one estate alone in Ardnamurchan, more than fifty crofters enrolled at the inaugural meeting of the local branch of the League; and the feeling of that first meeting was one of firm opposition to the payment of rent, until such times as its demands were met. The Duke of Argyll had recently refused to meet a delegation from the crofters of Tiree, or even to consider their demands; at the meeting held to consider his response, His Grace was the subject of 'adverse criticism of an extremely acrimonious character ... Much dissatisfaction was expressed in somewhat violent language ... A large number of rents due at Martinmas last are still unpaid and as His Grace has now expressed his resolution to enforce payment, the outlook at the present time is very dark. At the meeting, several of those who had paid their rents since last meeting were treated with scant courtesy, their actions being very markedly disapproved of'. The Valtos and Glendale men were released from gaol in Portree, their bail put up by the League; while in Kilmuir, the subscription, launched among the gentry to raise the £2,000 which was the minimum needed to prevent severe destitution there, closed, having failed to raise half that sum. In Lewis, eight crofters recently released from gaol for land agitation activities were again served with summonses for deforcement, land occupation, and breach of the peace. Meanwhile, Court of Session decrees were being issued against the owners of the cattle which grazed on an increasing number of islands in the sea lochs of Lewis; and others were issued at the same time against the tenants of the island of Bernera. In Portree Sheriff Court the landlord of Kilmuir was taking action against the Rev Davidson and nineteen others, for alleged destruction of estate dykes and fences, and the seizure of grazings belonging to himself.

In Sutherland, too, the agitation grew apace. In the third week of February delegates from all over the county packed the Free Church at Lairg, despite the snow and severe cold, to continue the business lately considered at an earlier conference in Helmsdale—parliamentary representation, policy on land law reform, and the foundation of a united Sutherland County Land League. In the chair that night at Lairg was the Loth delegate George MacLeod; and on the platform with him, sat the ministers of Assynt, Dornoch, Rogart and Altnaharra, and Dr Clarke, the crofters' candidate for Caithness. Apologies were received from Angus Sutherland of Glasgow, the Rev Cumming of Melness, and the Rev Mackenzie of Farr, who telegrammed to say that all the Reay country from Hope to Halladale was in favour of the conference and its business, and wished success to the agitation. Those present included delegates from Helmsdale, Creich, Loth, Dornoch, Rogart, Rosehall, Bonar and Gruids, together with five hundred local crofters and cottars. All enthusiastically supported the motion of Dr Clarke that, in the opinion of the meeting, no settlement of the Highland land question could be satisfactory unless it legally recognised the historic rights of the Highland people to the soil of their native land, and fixed 'the people on the soil under conditions just and equitable to all'.

Thus threatened by the organisation and unity of the people, the landlords of Sutherland resorted, as was happening elsewhere, to concession. The Duke himself believed concession to be expedient in the circumstances, and as his contribution offered to the people of Strathy 15,000 acres of a neighbouring sheep-farm—land from which their forefathers had been cleared. The people were less than impressed. As teacher George MacLeod told the Lairg conference: 'The landlords are now found making certain concessions—but why? It is simply to maintain the hold which they already have upon the people. Beware of the blandishments of the oppressors of the past from whom concessions are wrung and only made when they can no longer be denied'. The members of another branch of the League concurred with the Sutherland men in their assessment of the concessions offered by the landlords: assembling from Kishorn, Lochcarron, Easter Strome, Slumbay, Plockton, Jeantown and Mid-Strome, the members of the Lochcarron branch met to demand the land for the people, universal recognition of what they believed to be their inalienable right to it, and a just sufficiency of it for each. They condemned a minister's recent pronouncements on the land laws, in which it had been contended that 'Mosaic land laws were but ill-adapted to the present state of society, and that God had never intended them to apply to our times'. The branch president offered as refutation an interpretation of the second chapter of Habakkuk, verses 6-14, declared the matter solved and the minister concerned unfit to interpret the Scriptures, and closed the meeting with a benediction on the League and an appeal for continued agitation till their demands were met.

The Duke of Argyll (who also favoured concession, if coercion would not work) had described men like these as being possessed of 'incredible stupidity'. His son, the Marquis or Lorne, had similar opinions. Earlier that winter Donald MacFarlane had spoken to a strongly pro-crofter public meeting in Stepney; and in February, the tinplate workers of Thomas Glover's factory in Clerkenwell wrote to Lord Lorne on behalf of the Crofters' Defence Fund, noting that he was soon to become a member of the City Guild of Tinsmiths, and asking him for a donation to the crofters' legal defence fund. From his Kensington home, the Marquis counselled the tinplate workers not to subsidise or assist unconstitutional and cowardly attacks on the rights of property, or encourage acts of lawlessness.

By March, Lochcarron had become a stronghold of the League. Across the Sound of Raasay, in Portree, the Glendale and Valtos men seized by the marines and police force were about to stand trial; and in Inverness, moves were afoot to free the imprisoned Lewis crofters from gaol. In Mingary, the Ardnamurchan branch met under the presidency of Donald MacPhee; the meeting supported the adoption of Donald MacFarlane as the crofters' candidate for Argyll in the next parliamentary election, demanded the use of the local schools for League meetings, and reiterated their earlier decision that the people of the district would pay no more rent until their demands were met. The same day, the Lismore branch of the League met in Bachuil church under the presidency of the Rev Livingston, to denounce diminution of holdings, high rents, insecurity of tenure and want of compensation for improvements; and joined with Ardnamurchan in an appeal to MacFarlane to stand for Argyll at the next parliamentary election. In South Uist the people of Stoneybridge, Benbecula and Locheynort were warned by telegram that a Court of Session messenger was on his way with writs relating to the seizure of the landlord's land; when they reached Stoneybridge the messenger and his party were deforced and driven from the place; and the procurator-fiscal was engaged to identify the crime and the culprits. In Lochcarron, a crowded League meeting demanded land law reform at once, resolved that no landlord was fit to represent crofters in Parliament, and on hearing John Maclean of Jeantown tell how his father had been sent to prison for having had a net in the sea within a mile and a half of the River Carron, resolved unanimously to protest against the exclusive rights claimed by proprietors to salmon and trout fishing in the firths and rivers of Scotland. In Lewis, a depuation from the townships in the parish of Lochs delivered to Lady Matheson's residence a copy of the resolution passed by a meeting of the Lochs crofters—its tone one that was now familiar in the Highlands. The meeting, it ran, deeply regretted that Lady Matheson had not deemed it her duty to answer the petition and statements sent her from the townships to the south of Loch Erisort, or shown any desire to remove the grievances under which the crofters laboured: 'this meeting is of the opinion that no rent should be paid by the crofters until a satisfactory reply has been received'. From Lady Matheson, no reply was received; and from the crofters of Lochs, no rent was forthcoming.

Meanwhile, in Stornoway, nine men of Valtos and Kneep, arrested by the police and marine expedition in December, appeared in the Sheriff Court, charged with deforcement, obstruction, assault and breach of the peace. The previous autumn, crofters in the townships of Uig, Kneep and Tobson had seized lands cultivated by one of Lady Matheson's large farmers. Her Ladyship raised the matter in the Court of Session, and a messenger-at-arms was sent north to serve summonses. He succeeded in serving a number, until he arrived at the house in Valtos of the widow Catherine MacLeod, one of the crofters named as being involved in illegal grazing of stock on the seized lands. Those now in court, in the company of a large number of unruly persons unknown, placed themselves across the widow's door and prevented the serving of the summonses on her. Similar action was undertaken at another two houses in the district, thus leading to deforcement; and shortly afterwards, the messenger-at-arms claimed, he and his party were stoned and pelted with mud, and chased by the accused along the Meavaig road, and subjected all the time to abusive and violent language and threats.

Now, in February, the trial of these young crofters and fishermen's sons was due to begin; and though the roads in the interior of Lewis were all but impassable with snow, many crofters had walked in from long distances to be present. All day long the Court House was crowded, and the door besieged by crowds of people anxious to gain admittance. The messenger-at-arms, George Nicolson of Edinburgh, told how he had visited Lewis the previous year, and served thirty or so summonses in Valtos without interruption. 'I began my work at Brenish,' he told the packed court room, 'about ten miles from Valtos, and from there proceeded to Aird, Uig'. He had spent three days in that parish, then passed into Valtos, and then proceeded to Kneep, to serve summonses on Widow MacLeod, Angus Morrison and John Matheson. At the first house, fifty men prevented his entry; 'some one of the crowd came forward and held both his hands up to my face. He did not strike me, but he would not allow me to proceed further'. He understood from the attitudes and gestures of the men that it would be useless for him to attempt to force entry, and he considered it injudicious to quarrel with about fifty men. He finally threw his

129

summonses at the door of the widow's house, over the heads of the crowd; they were at once seized and trampled, and he saw no more of them. Nicolson and his assistant tried again at the other two houses, and were received with similar tactics, a pitcher of water being thrown from the roof of the third house; they were then chased to the temporary shelter of the schoolhouse, some 300 yards distant, where they fled upstairs. 'I remained about three-quarters of an hour in the schoolhouse, and when I came out to come away, I discovered the crowd was still lurking about. They rose about me like a flock of birds, and I was compelled to take refuge again. Altogether, I had to stay in the schoolhouse for about an hour, and then went safely on ... The people who were crying and hooting all the time spoke Gaelic, and of course I could not understand them'.

Nicolson's companion, Lady Matheson's ground officer for the parish of Uig, then gave evidence, which differed little from that of the messenger-at-arms. He told too of the flight to the schoolhouse, their temporary refuge in it, and their escape therefrom towards the manse, where a carriage was to meet them; and of how some people rolled boulders down on them from some considerable height. 'I was frightened they would injure me,' he confessed; 'it was in no friendly spirit that the mob was seeing us out of the township'.

Effectively, that closed the evidence for the prosecution; the defendants appeared next, and the court satisfied itself that none of them could read the language, far less understand the terminology of the summonses, Sheriff Black observing that perhaps ninety-five of every hundred witnesses who appeared in that court could speak only Gaelic, and required the services of an interpreter. The first witness took the stand; the sheriff warned him that, considering the evidence against him was given by no less a man than a messenger-at-arms of the Court of Session in Edinburgh, he had better be careful in what he denied. Angus MacLeod's agent warned the sheriff not to threaten his client; at which there was prolonged applause from the public gallery. The sheriff warned that if there was any other manifestation of feeling like this, he would clear the court; and this time, there was prolonged laughter from the public benches. Then the crofters' agent announced that the libel against his clients had been wrongly dated: the offence, as all the papers in the case showed, had been committed on 8th December, whilst the libel dated the incident on 8th November; the respectable and responsible prosecution witness had, in fact, blithely testified to having done in November what he had initially claimed to have done in December! The sheriff adjourned the case so that he might, as he put it, have an opportunity to look into the authorities on the matter.

By the following morning, the date on the libel had simply been changed. The sheriff talked of terrorism and robbery and rebellion by the Highland crofters—during the course of which remarks, the Rev MacIver marched from the witness box and left the court, having indignantly repudiated what he described as the sheriff's imputations against the people. That concluded the defence; the procurator and the crofters' agent spoke; and then Sheriff Black summed up. He began by suggesting that the bodily infirmities of the crofters' agent accounted for his peculiarities, and his odd and outrageous beliefs on the land question. For an hour and more he continued, speaking not on the case, but on the land agitation in general—of the Lewis crofters' arrogance and universal inclination to terrorism and cowardly bullying of elderly ladies of gentle spirit like Lady Matheson. Discontent, said the sheriff, was rampant, and in some areas anarchy reigned supreme. The landlord was now robbed of his rent, the sportsmen of his land, the law officer of his authority. Terrorism of individuals was everywhere manifest. Boycotting was painfully in evidence: sportsmen were boycotted, 'well-disposed' crofters were boycotted, landlords were boycotted. Numerous attempts at murder had been in evidence on the island—cowardly attempts, whereby stones were heaped on the roadways in the hope that some passing carriage would be overturned. Vicious and threatening letters had been sent, one to Lady Matheson herself, depicting a coffin and bearing the legend, 'Lady Matheson 1885'. In Stornoway itself there was a disgraceful degree of support for the agrarian lawlessness, many of those who should know better being evilly disposed towards the landlords. He did not believe that as many as half a dozen of the townsmen would sign a memorial denouncing the land agitation, were it to be hawked from the top of the town to the bottom. How sad to think that even in Stornoway the reign of terror was now complete! He, however, would not succumb; and he found the crofters guilty and gaoled them, refusing to accept fines as punishment (since they would be paid for by the Land League), and ordering the immediate arrest of anyone who should indicate any feeling when he gave sentence. John MacAulay was sentenced to fifty days' imprisonment and Donald Morrison was sent down for forty. These sentences, however, served only to stimulate even greater agitation than before, and not, as once would have been the case, a sullen and resigned silence.

Within a fortnight the resolve of the landless and land-hungry was concentrated further by a quite separate occurrence—the terrible fate of the men of the Ness and Broadbay fishing fleets. The cod-and ling-lining boats of both ports were caught at sea in a severe nor'easterly gale, out on the banks about fifteen miles offshore. Two boats ran to Cunndal Bay, hove-in, beached well-off, rolled, swamped and broke-up, and their crews were carried by the backwash to the deep water and lost. In Eoropie, nine widows and twenty-two orphans were left behind; and in Ness, six widows, and fifteen children. Their small open boats were no match for such conditions; and it was no consolation for the bereaved that no less an authority than Lord Napier's Royal Commission had recommended the provision of bigger boats for crofter-fishermen. In fact, the Government had yet to legislate on any of the Commission's proposals; and this inactivity itself fanned the resentment and impatience of those who suffered by it.

In the same way, the Commission had recommended action to remove defects in the administration of justice in the Highlands; and these defects were nowhere more obvious than in the Sheriff Court in Stornoway. On the morning when the Rev MacIver stormed from the court, Sheriff Black had already gaoled a number of Stornoway carpenters for mobbing one of Lady Matheson's associates. Within a week of those sentences Charles Cameron was denouncing them as a 'miscarriage of justice' in the House of Commons; and a public meeting in Stornoway was demanding a public inquiry into the administration of justice in the Highlands in general. The Stornoway meeting resolved to petition the Home Secretary for the release of the gaoled men; copies were sent to the Lord Advocate, and Fraser-Mackintosh was alerted to the matter. Harcourt calmly returned the petition to the procurator-fiscal in Stornoway for his comments; but the Valtos men were out of gaol within a fortnight, temporarily freed by a High Court order while the authorities deliberated on the justice, or expediency, of enforcing the sentences. This campaign, and its outcome, did not go unnoticed in Skye, where Sheriff Ivory was now ready to begin his trial of the men of Glendale and Valtos.

The land before them

'A majority of 2017!
When we first heard the fact
proclaimed, and reflected on what
it meant and implied, our thoughts
involuntarily ran into the mould
of thought and feeling imbedded
in the grand old Psalm of
Deliverance ... applicable
not only to the crofter population
at present, but in its main features
to the emancipated of every name, of
every colour, and of every clime'.

The Invergordon Times

'Nemesis has overtaken
the landlords of the Highlands,
and we not sorry.
We are glad'.

The Oban Times

In March, 1885, the Glendale and Valtos men appeared in Portree Sheriff Court. The seven men from Glendale were charged with mobbing and rioting, assault on an officer of the law, and breach of the peace. According to the indictment, they had, 'all and each or one or more of them, along with a mob or great number of riotous and evil-disposed persons, of which all and each or one or more of the accused formed a part, in riotous and tumultuous manner, and in breach of the public peace and to the alarm of the lieges', assembled upon the high road which led from Holmisdal, where they had met 'for the unlawful purpose of preventing by force the service of the said summonses'. The prosecution further alleged that the mob had, by force, violence, imprecations and threats, prevented the service of writs, and within the schoolhouse at Colbost assaulted a number of legal officers engaged in their duty, and struck them several blows with their fists and with clods of earth, 'and did trip them, and kick them and knock them or one or more of them down on the ground several times'; moreover, that they had by force and violence prevented sheriff-officer Grant from serving his summonses, he having been driven, pushed, shoved, and kicked by a great number of riotous and evilly-disposed persons—the accused and their associates, it was alleged—a distance of five miles along the road, in the course of which he was forced to destroy his papers.

From the packed public benches, John MacPherson and the Rev MacCallum listened to the sheriff-officer tell the court how he had gone by mail-cart from Portree to Dunvegan, and thence by dog-cart into Glendale, collecting two assistants on the way. On foot now, they met no trouble for some time, until, at two o'clock in the afternoon, they called on the house of Widow Mackinnon, where they were to serve their summonses. The widow dashed the papers to the ground, said Grant, and called her son, now one of the accused in court, who came out and pinioned Grant, saying, 'You come in here till I get the neighbours gathered together to see what you are about'. At this the widow yelled and jeered at him, crying that soon the people would rise, and asking her son why no horns had yet sounded in the glen, and were all the menfolk all asleep? The sheriff officer broke free, and started to lead his little party back the way they had come. But men were now appearing with sticks; by the time they reached the post office there were already twenty of them, and as they crossed the bridge horns were sounding across the glen. Grant's assistant, Macleod, took refuge, uninvited, in the bedroom of the schoolhouse, just above Mr Davies' classroom; the crowd, now hundreds strong, pursued him there, and dragged him out, notwithstanding his attempts to cling to Mr and Mrs Davies' iron bedstead. Mr Davies himself told the court later that the disturbance was 'very unsettling' for his scholars.

At this point, unexpectedly, the defence and the prosecution announced an agreement: five of the seven would be found not guilty, if two of their number would plead guilty to mobbing and rioting. Two did, and were sentenced to three weeks' imprisonment, a sentence absurd in its leniency by the standards of the day. The court, however, did not dare to impose more than token sentences, which did not impress the crofters in the slightest. As one report of the case put it, 'The trial is creating quite as much interest as those at Stornoway did a few weeks ago; and, it is almost needless to add, the sympathy of the people of the district is entirely with the men who are to be tried'.

When the three Valtos men appeared in court, on the following Friday at ten in the morning, popular sympathy for the accused was equally strong. One was but a boy, and one an old man; while the third crofter, Norman Stewart, was a keen Land Leaguer and a man known throughout Skye as 'Parnell'. The sheriff could not find much grounds to convict them on the charge of mobbing and rioting, or indeed of assault and breach of the peace, until he recalled the strictures of Lord Cockburn in the High Court in Inverness some forty years before; if any one of the accused was in a mob, then he or she must take responsibility for everything done by that mob, for 'a man in a mob is only safe by joining the authorities'. Thus reassured, Sheriff Speirs sent the young boy to gaol for ten days and released the other two, 'Parnell' and Murdoch MacDonald. They were met outside the court-house by a great crowd of fellow-crofters from Kilmuir, who set out to walk home with them, through the night, by the tracks that led into the northern peninsula of the island.

In his final remarks, Sheriff Speirs had warned the crofters, 'You must see that the authorities mean business, and will not allow any form of lawlessness to go on'. But despite the sheriff's protestations, this was precisely what the authorities were allowing, for the simple reason that they were powerless to prevent it—as Alexander Mackenzie clearly understood, when he wrote that the results of both trials gave general satisfaction, and that such a ludicrous wind-up to Sheriff Ivory's foolish police and military expedition to Skye was 'convincing proof of that gentleman's unfitness for presiding over the judicial affairs of the County of Inverness'. A month earlier, commenting on the Stornoway trials, Mackenzie had written similarly of Sheriff Black's 'general exhibition' of his unfitness for the judicial office he held; on that occasion he proceeded to castigate the method of appointing legal officials in the Highlands, declaring that it was deplorable in the extreme that men, whose only qualification was that they were 'paupers upon the bounty of their Trade Guild', should be placed in positions of power and trust, to dispense justice. The district in which such a man dispensed justice, or what passed for such, soon lost confidence in him, and in doing so, lost confidence in the administration of justice in the country. When this feeling took possession of a community, 'acts of what are called lawlessness appear to the people their only method of asserting their rights; and when a community once starts on a course of lawless conduct, there is no saying where it may stop'.

In April, three crofters from South Uist were fined for deforcement and breach of the peace. Later in the same month thirteen men from Waternish were gaoled at Portree for mobbing and rioting on the occasion of sheriff

135

officer Grant's visit to their district; and, on the very day they were sentenced, a party of messengers from the Court of Session was reported to be on a new trip to Lewis at the bidding of Lady Matheson. On the mainland, too, lawlessness was rife, and spreading; but now the Government, and the forces of authority in general, were belatedly coming to recognise the truth of Mackenzie's analysis of that lawlessness; and at last Westminster prepared to act, in order to bring about a settlement of the land agitation. Practically every member of the political and social Establishment now saw the need for social peace in the Highlands; and the necessity of substantial legislated concessions, as the price of that peace, was recognised by all—by all, that is, except the Highland proprietors themselves. This time, however, they were summarily over-ruled; for within a fortnight of the Waternish gaolings the Lord Advocate was asking leave of the House of Commons to introduce a Bill on the subject.

The decision to legislate, Mackenzie wrote triumphantly, was a remarkable acknowledgement of the justice of the claims of the Highland people, 'and a complete justification of all that has been urged by ourselves and other advocates of reform ... and particularly so, when it is remembered how, only two or three years ago, the Lord Advocate, speaking for the Government, declared in the House of Commons that the crofters had no grievances to speak of and that there was not the slightest necessity for inquiry or legislation'. Mackenzie himself had travelled to London to hear, from the gallery of the Commons, the Bill's introduction by the Lord Advocate; he admitted later to having 'experienced a degree of pleasure' on hearing the speech. The discussion following the Lord Advocate's speech lasted until three in the morning; the Bill itself was published on the following Wednesday, when the Government's proposals were made public for the first time. The landlords did not like them; the sentiments of one island landlord, expressed in the London *Times*, was still characteristic of their traditional response. The Napier Commission, he wrote, had been a farce, and full of partiality, and the proper remedy was emigration. No honest and impartial person, in perusing the evidence of the Napier Commission Report could fail to be struck by the 'extreme kindness and leniency' with which the crofters everywhere had been treated by the landowners in the Highlands and Islands of Scotland. These islands of the north were in perfect peace, and 'goodwill subsisted everywhere between landlords and tenants' before the appointment of the Royal Commission. Since then, however, 'everything had been tried to sow discord between classes ... To carry out the demands that have been put into the crofters' mouths would throw the Highlands and Islands back one hundred years'. The Bill was a bare-faced bid for the vote of the new electorate, enfranchised by the electoral reform of the previous year; and was designed to win their support, 'by pandering to their covetousness and worst passions'.

As the landlords mobilised privately, in the corridors of political power, to resist the Government's proposals, some preliminary salvoes were fired

John Stewart of Valtos, with crofters from Major Fraser's estate—'matters have now come to crisis in this district.'

in public. The Duke of Argyll denounced the Lord Advocate's suggestion, made in his introductory speech on the proposals, that in pre-commercial days, in the old clan times, the people had partial right in the ownership of the land. The landlords, declared Argyll, owned the land absolutely, and had always done so. Major Fraser of Kilmuir maintained that emigration was still the only remedy, claiming that the legislation was quite worthless. Writing from Brook's Club in London, Lord Lovat proclaimed his belief that the Bill would confer little benefit on the crofter, 'while it introduces the thin end of the wedge which, driven home, will revolutionise the system of landed property through the whole country'. The effect of the Bill, in his opinion, would be to deprive the landlord of his 'chief interest' in the property, and he would 'no longer' take any interest in the improvement of his property or the 'assistance of his people.' The Bill would be the hardest blow yet struck at landed proprietors in Great Britain; and, he concluded, 'neither is it an honest blow given in fair fight'.

The Bill did not satisfy Alexander Mackenzie either, as he made clear in the *Times*, in the *Celtic Magazine*, and in his new agitational paper the

137

Scottish Highlander. The principle of the Bill was 'a long step in the right direction'; but its specific proposals were of little practical value, and in some instances were worse than useless. Any legislation which did not make provision for the acquisition of more land by the crofters could not and would not satisfy the Highland people; 'for a Bill which does not provide for the compulsory breaking down of the large sheep-farms and deer-forests will never be accepted as a measure of redress nor satisfy those who have been so harshly treated by the evicting landlords of the past'. The Bill had been whittled down till it was so nearly worthless that he believed the rumour, then current, that the only people consulted by the Government at its drafting stage were Lochiel and the other organisers of the Inverness Proprietors' Conference. Mackenzie added, however, that 'a Bill which is opposed by the *Scotsman*, the Duke of Argyll, and Major Fraser of Kilmuir cannot be altogether bad, either in principle or effect'.

In the event, however, the Bill was never subjected to the further trials of a passage through the House of Commons or, more particularly, through the House of Lords. It was, in effect, substantially similar in its provisions to the Irish Land Act of four years earlier; and it would clearly have faced uncompromising resistance in the Lords. But in June Gladstone's Government went out of office, and Lord Salisbury formed a new Government, which, despite Mackenzie's expectations, chose not to implement the Bill, and dropped it from its schedule.

In the Highlands, the agitation, which had lapsed briefly on the introduction of the Bill, was, naturally enough, renewed with vigour. Samuel and Alice Cameron from Drimarben were fined for assault arising from their attempts to defend themselves against the due process of law. Five of Lady Cathcart's crofting tenants from South Uist were arraigned before the Court of Session in Edinburgh; they were treated leniently, according to the Lord President, and gaoled for a month. In August, Donald MacArthur of Kilmuir, who was alleged to have helped to deforce the sheriff-officers in March, was arrested in Perthshire, where he was working as a labourer. He was taken to Portree, and committed to gaol. Bail of £30 was raised at once; and when this had secured his release, £5 was quickly gathered by the guests in the Portree Hotel and presented to him to 'alleviate his destitute circumstances'. From Lewis it was reported that in the absence of their husbands and brothers at the fishing, 'the women of the neighbourhood are holding their own and carrying out the warfare vigorously'. In Uig, when two of Lady Matheson's large farmers attempted to put cattle on the islands seized the previous year by the crofters, the local women blinded the men with sand, and stampeded the cattle with sticks and stones. At Linshader the byre belonging to a crofter who insisted on working for the estate authorities was fired during the night. In South Shawbost two hundred yards of dyke, built to exclude the crofters' stock, were completely demolished. In Shawbost, too, a sheriff-officer who had been sent to confiscate furniture from a croft house was met by a crowd of women hurling sticks and stones, forcing him and his party to beat a hasty retreat.

138

In the south, the agitation in the Highlands had another effect, as the sporting season for grouse and stag and salmon grew near. In the London office of Lumley's the estate agents, in fashionable St James's, no less than half a million pounds' worth of Highland sporting land was up for sale, on estates all over the Highlands, from Aberdeenshire to Wester Ross. But whether the owners had set their sights too high, or whether potential buyers had grown newly cautious, the bidding was distinctly sluggish, and in general the desire to own Highland estates—and Highland tenants— was not keen. Sir Duff Gordon's baronial domain of Fyvie in Aberdeenshire, with 11,000 acres, a magnificent castle, and an annual income from rent of over £8,000, failed to raise a bid of more than £260,000; at which price Duff Gordon was disinclined to sell. Certainly, the Wyvis deer forest was sold, to a Mr Schoolbred of Tottenham Court Road; but the top offer of £64,000 for Pittodrie, with its 3,000 acres of Aberdeenshire, imposing residence and £2,500 rent-roll, was not acceptable to the sellers. No offers at all were made for Strathkyle in Ross-shire, with its 2,000 acres of grouse-moors; or for Mingary in Argyll with its 23,000 sporting acres, its valuable fisheries—and its thriving Land League branch; or for the excellent accommodation and wide acres of Invercharron-in-the-Craigs in Ross-shire. In Aberdeenshire the Dun Echt estate was on offer at £200,000, comprising 9,000 of the very best sporting acres, an annual rental income of £5,000, valuable timber plantations, and Dun Echt House, upon which Lord Crawford and Balcarres had recently spent £100,000 in improvements. But the Dun Echt estate was also withdrawn from offer. The Stirkirke estate, with 7,000 acres, a large mansion, and an income from rent of £3,000 annually, was also withdrawn by its owners when the highest bid did not exceed £65,000. In Ross-shire the Ben Damph lands, with the best fishing and shooting in the country, were withdrawn from sale too, when no offer over £40,000 was received. And in Inverness-shire the Glen Gloy sporting estate, close to Fort Augustus, failed to reach its reserve price of £28,000, though it boasted 4,500 acres and a fine residence from which to survey them, and though Lumley's auctioneer had been able to say, when recapitulating the 'attractions of the estate', that 'it possesses neither tenants, paupers, nor crofters, is well stocked with all kinds of game, and will afford constant sport for the lover of the rod and the gun'.

But although the Glen Gloy estate was happily free of such distractions as tenants, paupers and crofters, there were nevertheless many of them remaining across the Highlands; and at the beginning of September nearly two hundred of their delegates assembled for what had now become the annual conference of the League. They met in Portree, under the presidency of Fraser-Mackintosh, and the conference comprised not only delegates representing every area of the Highlands, from the counties of Argyll, Caithness, Sutherland, Ross and Inverness, and the islands, but also representatives and visitors from the United States, Canada, New Zealand, and Australia, and a host of the crofters' supporters and

Glen Tilt deer-forest in Perthshire. Robert Somers wrote of it in the middle of the nineteenth century—'The Clearance system was begun here long before it was thought of in many other parishes. Whatever merit Mr James Loch and Mr Patrick Sellar may take to themselves for expelling the people from the straths of Sutherlandshire, they cannot claim the merit of originality... Glen Tilt was cleared of its inhabitants by the present Duke of Atholl's grandfather, twenty or thirty years before the burnings and ejectments of Sutherland were heard of.'

The drawing-room of Mar Shooting Lodge. 'A deer-forest is beginning to be considered as a necessary appendage of an estate. If it wants that, it wants dignity...', wrote Robert Somers in the *North British Daily Mail.*

spokesmen in Parliament, including MacFarlane, MacCallum, John Mackay of Hereford, MacPherson, Mackenzie, Sutherland and Clarke. Clarke reported to the conference that the national offices in Edinburgh and London had now determined to liaise even more closely than before; and that there were now, not counting local and county associations, near to 130 branches of the League, with as many as 14,000 members in those branches alone. John Anderson, a delegate from Stornoway, reminded the conference that many branches had organised several sub-branches. In Stornoway, he said, there had been weekly meetings all through the previous winter and spring, well-attended by crofters from all parts of Lewis; and ten sub-branches had been formed, including the ones at Carloway, Back and Sandwick. Branches were also being formed, said Clarke, in New Zealand and America; and in the south they had used every means, addressing public meetings and employing all recognised modes of agitation, 'to educate public opinion up to the mark; and they were in every way satisfied with their results'. Should it be considered necessary, there would be no difficulty in rousing 50,000 men to parade through London to show their support for the crofters' cause, he went on; and before long their wrongs would be righted and the day of the oppressors, the lairds and the factors who had tyrannised and oppressed the poor crofters, would soon be at an end. John MacLeod, one of the Sutherland delegates, reported that there were twenty-one branches in operation in his area, and that the people there were now so well organised that the landlords did not dare attempt to evict anyone. Thomas MacDonald, from Inverness-shire, speaking of the effects of the agitation in his own district, said that it had almost entirely thrown-off the nightmare of landlordism and had completely broken the power of estate officialdom over the people; and one of the Argyll representatives, the Rev MacDonald, maintained that the crofting people were now done with landlords and landlordism.

The next speaker, Alexander Morrison from Lewis, said that the people had been kept down in poverty and oppression for centuries through unjust and cruel land laws manufactured by the people's oppressors—the landlords; what the people demanded, said Morrison, was the compulsory division of all deer-forests, sheep-farms and large farms into crofts and small-holdings, according to the requirements of the population in each district throughout the Highlands and Islands. He demanded fair rents, durability of tenure, compensation for improvements, a land court, and the abolition of the game-laws. Malcolm Steel from North Uist and John MacQueen from South Uist spoke next; then John MacPherson of Glendale, John Murdoch, and the Rev MacGregor of Chicago, who was received with great applause, the audience rising en masse and waving their hats to cheer his promise of the full support of the expatriate Highlanders of North America. Stuart Glennie deplored the fact that fifty men could own—'as their own private parks'—two million acres of the country. Mr Picton, MP, told of an earlier visit to Loch Duich, where he had seen the shameful sight of wide, rich, deserted lands, the fields fenced in with stone walls, and no one allowed to enter, because the land was a deer-forest. Donald MacFarlane owned to the same abhorrence of deer-forests, and expressed his agreement with the delegate from Lewis who had demanded the abolition of the game laws. 'Every man who goes down to the sea and puts his net into it,' he declared, to ringing applause, 'has the right to take out of it what God Almighty has put into it.' Dr Clarke reported that in the previous year, the League had spent £300 on the legal defence of crofters and the support of their families, and though they had still £100 in hand, more money must be collected for the legal defence fund, 'in view of the oppression and tyranny that is likely to be exercised by the landlords in the Highlands during the coming winter'; at once, donations amounting to £50 were pledged.

Clearly, the crofters' movement was on the offensive; and this was MacFarlane's theme when, in the afternoon session, he introduced the first major motion of the day by declaring that, whereas they called this a conference of delegates, he called it a council of war. Could anyone who had observed the agitation in the Highlands deny that there had been an enormous advance since their meeting last year in Dingwall? There was no use in attempting to negotiate with the landlords, he declared to cheers. It was too late for negotiation. Thereupon the conference unanimously condemned as inadequate the proposals of the Government's Bill of some months previously, and reiterated its demands for fair rents, security, compensation, and a land court. It went on, moreover, to demand the wholesale expropriation of the Highland landlords, 'restoring to town-ships the grazings of which they have been robbed, and to the community generally the benefits to be derived from the said forests, moorlands, and hill-grazings'; and it resolved 'to continue the agitation for Highland land reform till such a measure as above indicated becomes law'.

The conference closed at six in the evening; two hours later, the delegates attended a post-conference meeting, with representatives of the English Land Restoration League, the Scottish Land League of America, and the Scottish Land Restoration League in attendance. The speakers were from Skye, Chicago, London, Hull, Caithness, Glasgow, Edinburgh, Oban, Liverpool, Hereford, and Barra—the last mentioned being Michael Buchanan, who had also been a delegate to the Dingwall conference the previous year.

The following day three thousand people gathered to parade through Portree in a 'demonstration which may be said without exaggeration to be the largest and most important meeting that has taken place since the land agitation commenced'. Many of the crofters had travelled all night to attend, walking between twenty and twenty-five miles, from Dunvegan and Waternish and Kilmuir. At ten in the morning the Portree contingent went out to meet the men of Uig and Staffin, and returned with them to Portree just as the Braes and Sconser contingent arrived, with pipes and flags, and banners proclaiming 'The Land for the People', 'Shoulder to Shoulder', and 'The Earth He hath Given to the Children of Men'. For all of six hours, at their meeting-place behind the Caledonian Bank, the crowd heard these slogans amplified by Murdoch, MacPherson, MacCallum, Mackenzie, Sutherland, MacFarlane and Fraser-Mackintosh. On the platform sat three Members of Parliament, a host of prospective parliamentary candidates, many of the best-known land-reformers in Britain, and no less than seven clergymen, as MacCallum drew on the examples of Lazarus and the rich man, and of Pharaoh and the children of Israel, to depict social relations in the Highlands, and particularly in his former parish of Arisaig—where, he ventured to suggest, Pharaoh still ruled.

The most important business of the conference, however, had been to appoint a group of pro-crofter spokesmen to contest the Highland constituencies on the programme of the Land League at the earliest opportunity. With only two votes cast against, the conference accepted as crofter-candidates, on an explicitly anti-landlord platform: for Inverness-shire, Fraser-Mackintosh; for Argyll, Donald MacFarlane; for Ross-shire, Dr Roderick Macdonald; for Caithness, Dr Clarke; and for Sutherland-shire, Angus Sutherland. From the moment that the demonstration concluded, the crofters' candidates began their campaigns, which were, in each case, based explicitly on the demands of the League.

To the landlords these demands were unworthy even of contempt. Voicing their fervent belief, the *Scotsman* editorialised: 'If we are not to break up our whole social system ... the demands of the conference at Portree must be set aside as monstrous and utterly inadmissible'. A few days later the same paper added that the 'incendiarism' of the conference had merely 'held out a bribe to the lawless to encourage and practise lawlessness'. The pro-crofter *Invergordon Times*, however, voiced another opinion when it called the programme 'pretty radical, considering the modest proposals offered a few months ago ... Now nothing short of the total abolition of deer-forests ... will satisfy the public demands'. If landlords had been half as wise as they got credit for, they would have restricted deer-forests within limits. Instead of this they had depopulated some of the most fertile straths in the country, and handed them over to 'heartless millionaires' who offered the highest rents, while the evicted people were huddled together in thousands on miserable patches of land by the seashore. 'For this reason, if for no other, would it be well to abolish deer-forests. Such candidates as Sir Kenneth Mackenzie and Novar, who are the owners of extensive deer-forests, will of course say that this is confiscation. As well to say that to oust landlords from Parliament is confiscation'. If the people would only use the present opportunity by returning the popular candidates by a crushing majority, they would be able, in a dozen years, to effect a satisfactory settlement, once and for all, of the land question. Were crofters to starve or leave the country, merely that a pampered aristocracy might revel in the dissipation of Modern Babylon? 'The god mammon must be dethroned ... The most gracious act the landlords could accomplish at the present time ... is to retire from the

143

present contest'. The same newspaper warned that the landlords and their agents would be certain to attempt to sabotage the votes of the crofters and the campaigns of their candidates, and urged any reader who knew of, or came upon, such sabotage, to report it to the secretary of the League; such an exposure would be useful; for it would serve to 'identify the determination of those whose long-suffering patience has already reached a high pitch of tension, and be calculated to embitter an agitation that is supported by grim resolution'.

In the teeming Partick district of Glasgow, with its high density of dispossessed Highlanders, John Murdoch was making ready to contest the next election there—with none other than the son of the late Patrick Sellar; while in the northern constituencies the contest was no less bitter, and no less clear-cut. In Helmsdale the Rev Cruickshank won tempestuous applause when he spoke passionately in the local church to urge support for the crofter candidate for Sutherland, and to commend steadfast resistance to tyranny and oppression. He cited passages from the history of Joseph to support his contention that 'the happy and prosperous condition of the children of Israel in the lands of Canaan, under divine law as laid down in the Scriptures, amply prove that God created the earth for the benefit of all His creatures and not for a pampered few ... The Highlanders were dispossessed of their just rights by scheming and treacherous aristocracy ... being made houseless and homeless, to be supplanted by sheep and deer in order that the pockets of the Duke of Sutherland might be better filled'. To place any confidence in the Marquis of Stafford, the minister suggested, was utterly absurd; he could see no good that the sitting Member had ever done in Parliament, and neither would he expect him ever to do any good 'from his social position and connection with the Duke of Argyll and his aristocratic ring'. On the other hand the crofters' candidate, Angus Sutherland, was possessed of great scholarly attainment, was a great authority on Highland affairs, would be of immense weight and influence in the House of Commons, and therefore deserved the support of every single crofter in the county.

Similar campaigns were developing in all the Highland constituencies. In Ross-shire, young Munro Ferguson of Novar kept his lawyers busy with objections to the inclusion of individual crofters on the electoral role; and at every public meeting he was confronted by supporters of Dr Macdonald, whose conduct there merely confirmed the suspicions Novar had recently disclosed to the Duke of Argyll. Novar was, in the words of the *Invergordon Times*, 'in alliance with all the ... lairds, big farmers, and land grabbers, with the view to throw reform into the far future, and to keep the people in the bonds of slavery'. In the same issue the paper noted that it had printed over 6,000 copies the previous week, its circulation having 'gone up by leaps and bounds during the last year. This shows that the cause we are advocating is the people's cause'.

In Inverness-shire, Argyll and Caithness the spirit was the same: at countless local League meetings the people agreed to support their crofter-

A deserted crofting settlement at Carsaig Bay, Argyll, photographed at the height of the land agitation. Few crofters involved in the agitation were unaware of the verse in Isaiah that reads 'Your country is desolate, your cities are burned with fire; your land, strangers devour it in your presence, and it is desolate, as overthrown by strangers'.

candidate, no matter what the landlord-candidate might say. In Lochcarron a packed League meeting agreed 'that as our land laws were originally framed by, and for the sole benefit of, the landowning class, the people are now determined to support no landlord-candidate however fair his promises, and that therefore every effort should be made by the crofters to further the interests of Dr Macdonald in his candidature'. In Argyll ministers favourable to the Duke denounced MacFarlane for having been a Member of Parliament for an Irish constituency. Throughout the constituency, however, League meetings enthusiastically declared their support for him; as he was to tell the House of Commons three months later, he had been handicapped in every possible way during the election, with the power of heavens and earth against him. The landlords were the earth and the ministers were the heavens. But although he was denounced by everybody, from the highest laird down to the smallest laird, by nearly all the ministers in every pulpit every day they were in it, the people showed their determination.

The pro-landlord press attacked the crofter-candidates mercilessly. To the *Scotsman* Dr Clarke, the Caithness candidate, was a mere carpet-

145

bagger quite unfit to contest the representation of the county with a man who had the 'high recommendation of having served with distinction in the Soudan'. In Inverness-shire, Fraser-Mackintosh was vilified by the *Inverness Courier* and the *Northern Chronicle*, which misrepresented his meetings in Arisaig and elsewhere. Copies of both papers were, reportedly, sent free to members of the electorate in the Beauly district; but when the crofter-candidate himself spoke there, in Kirkton schoolhouse, bonfires were made of the pro-landlord newspapers. A small meeting in Arisaig, chaired by Astley-Nicholson himself, heard Fraser-Mackintosh's opponent; on resuming his seat, he was accorded no more than a solemn and forbidding silence. In Ross-shire, too, the *Journal* vilified the crofter-candidate—unsurprisingly, perhaps, given that Munro Ferguson of Novar owned a substantial stake in the paper. The *Highland News* was no better, demonstrating for the crofter-candidates 'venom equal almost to the *Journal*'. In Sutherland the *Northern Ensign* was burned ceremoniously; it too had been sent free for distribution among the new voters, that they might read in its columns the letters and speeches in favour of the landlord-candidate, the Marquis of Stafford. It was twelve years since Fraser-Mackintosh had stood successfully for the town of Inverness; in those twelve years, what progress had been made had been achieved despite the overwhelmingly anti-crofter bias of the national and Highland press—with such honourable exceptions as the *Inverness Advertiser*, which had supported Fraser-Mackintosh from the start. Obstructions of all sorts still remained; as E R Macdonnell of Morar, one of Fraser-Mackintosh's sponsors in the election, told a meeting days before the poll, the new crofter voters of the district had been compelled to travel an eighty mile return journey to Fort William to register as voters. That so many had done so was an eloquent testimony to the strength of their political motivation. Pre-election meetings in Arisaig and Camusdarroch and Tougal all testified to the popular support for Fraser-Mackintosh in those places and on Lord Lovat's nearby estate, 'Mr Fraser-Mackintosh has no stauncher supporters than the electors of North Morar and Bracara'.

In December, as the results of the election slowly became known, the crofters were shown to have won a very great victory. Their candidates had won in Argyll, Inverness, Ross and Caithness; and had lost only in Sutherland, where the son of the Duke defeated Angus Sutherland. Alexander Mackenzie, writing in the *Scottish Highlander*, called the Sutherland result a victory for 'vile and subservient folly'; the results overall, however, led him to believe that 'the crofters' cause is advancing at an extraordinary and unexpected pace'. After the last general election these constituencies had been represented, respectively, by the Marquis of Lorne, Cameron of Lochiel, Alexander Matheson, Sinclair of Ulbster, and the Marquis of Stafford, who between them owned, or were heir to, nearly two million acres of land. The anti-crofter press and the landlords generally were horrified at this unexpected reverse, explaining the outrage and thanklessness of it all as due to the scheming mendacity of the crofters' candidates, and the ignorant greed of the newly-enfranchised electorate. The crofters, however, and the League, were justly exultant. 'The victory', reported the *Invergordon Times*, 'was hailed with great delight ... by the crofters, and bonfires blazed and general rejoicings took place'.

The contest had been a bitter one from beginning to end; for in it 'the upper classes saw their last hold of power slipping away from their grasp, and made the most desperate efforts to retain it'. In Ross-shire, Munro Ferguson and Dr Macdonald had both toured the constituency twice; neither an election nor electioneering of this kind had ever been seen before in the Highlands. The effect of all this on the mass of the people had been remarkable—as the result of the election bore witness. In the opinion of the *Invergordon Times*, 'to say that landlordism was beaten was not half the truth; it was trampled in the dust and had become an object of derision even to its former slaves.' For the landlords, the result was the 'most tremendous slap in the face'; and considering that the crofters had laboured under the great disadvantages of 'imperfect registration, enormous inconvenience as to polling places, and much timidity due to inexperience', it could be assumed 'with safety' that the people would go on to improve and strengthen their new position. And on the last day of the year the same newspaper repeated that the result had been a 'terrible defeat to the holders of the soil; ... all eyes are turned towards the new representatives ... At the same time we would take the liberty of reminding the constituencies that they also have their duty to perform, and that without agitation outside of Parliament, there can be none inside Parliament'.

The *Invergordon Times* need not have feared such a loss of momentum, however; for within weeks the agitation had recommenced, on an even greater scale than before. As the new year advanced, indeed, events across the Highlands were to validate the judgement of the *Oban Times*, which had commented on the results of the election becoming known: 'From the Mull of Kintyre to the Butt of Lewis, the land is before us'.

An instalment of justice

*'The land is our birthright, even
as the air, the light of the sun,
and the water belong to us as our
birthright'.*

DONALD MACCALLUM

On Tuesday 14th January, 1886, the new Members of Parliament were sworn in, the new Speaker was elected, and it was announced that the Queen's Speech would be delivered on the 21st. And as the new crofters' members planned the tactics they would employ within the Palace of Westminster, their electors, as the *Invergordon Times* had counselled, were keeping up the agitation in the country at large.

That same week the Alness branch of the League resolved that 'there must be no folding of the hands and no inaction for many years hence'. The members of the Creich branch resolved to defend William Black of Gruids from threatened eviction, debated the latest editorial of the *Oban Times* on the land question, and demanded more land and security of tenure; and they agreed enthusiastically that, now that they had their own men in Parliament, 'the landlords would very soon sit up'. At a League meeting in Melness, chaired by Donald MacPherson, ten new subscriptions to the *Invergordon Times* were taken out. The theme of MacPherson's speech was that the agitation must be continued, both at the fireside and at public meetings. No-one should be deceived by the recent local halving of rents, he maintained; this reduction, which had been announced just before the election, was merely a bribe to electors. A fifty per cent reduction was little, considering the rents they had been paying, over the last seventy years, for patches of land reclaimed by themselves; and MacPherson hoped that the people would soon show the Marquis of Stafford 'that they had been robbed of their natural rights, in their native soil, and that they would not be satisfied with less than a full restoration of the lands of which they had been deprived by fraud and usurpation'. In Clyne, local chairman Alexander Maclean told a Land League meeting that this was no time to stop agitating, but 'to go on increasing in vigour'; and the Kildonan branch resolved unanimously to continue the agitation, as no settlement of the land question would be satisfactory to the people of the Highlands which did not provide for the distribution of the land among the people, quite independently of the will of the landlords, and in such a way and on such terms, 'as will free the people from the social and political bondage in which they are at present held by the landlords'.

At a meeting of the Loth branch, Donald Mackay condemned as utterly futile the hope that the landlords would effect any improvement in their condition. The landlords had done everything in their power to exterminate them, he said, to root their race clear out of their native soil; and now that it suited their purpose, they would come forward 'in their cringing, fawning, hypocritical way, talking smoothly', while their hearts were 'full of the blackest and bitterest rage against the native race'. The policy of the landlords, he continued, was to degrade the people and keep them servile and submissive; but now he saw signs of a coming dawn—and for that they owed nothing to the landlords. Salvation could not come to them from that quarter, for the same fountain could not give forth bitter water and sweet—a truth they had 'on a higher authority than Dunrobin and all his lickspittles'. Donald Mackay was followed by Donald Gunn, who wholeheartedly echoed his sentiments. To Mackay and Gunn the no-rent movement in Skye was well-founded, just, and worthy of their support and emulation. But Skye was not nearly so badly off as Loth; if the Skye people had cause to withhold their rent, the people of Loth had tenfold cause. The meeting thereupon resolved unanimously to continue further support for the Gruids crofter, William Black, now under notice of eviction. The Rosehall men demanded a suspension of all evictions until such time as a parliamentary Act finally outlawed the practice, and resolved to carry on the fight to hasten that day. At a meeting of the Laid branch, many spoke of the shortage of land available to the people; it was decided to press for the breaking-up of the farm of Eriboll into smaller holdings; and it was agreed that, if the landlords refused to comply with the wants and wishes of the people, then 'they must take the consequences!' Of that meeting it was reported: 'There is a strong determination here to take forcible possession unless our rights are granted'. And the determination expressed in Laid was felt in every part of the country.

Golspie now had an increasingly active branch; and at the Stoer branch meeting, the following week, it was agreed to respond to an appeal from the Laid branch for assistance for William Black in his fight against eviction. Hugh MacLeod reminded his audience, to cheers, that the broker of the local sheep-farmers was recently bankrupted and had fled to Spain to avoid the legal consequences; the effect of this, said MacLeod, to louder cheers, would be the bankruptcy of the sheep-farmers themselves. And the chairman, Kenneth Mackenzie, urged his members to remain loyal to the League; the agitation must be kept stronger than ever, and they must all have their eyes on Parliament. That same week the Halladale branch demanded the restoration of the land to the people; and in Strathpeffer, the secretary of the local branch reminded its members that half the battle had still to be fought; it was their duty to endeavour to back up their friends in Parliament in any legislation that might be attempted for the benefit of the people. Donald MacDonald of Inchvanie noted that the Duchess of Sutherland was reducing her rents, but believed that the reductions offered were derisory. The meeting agreed; and resolved that the agitation must go on. In Garve, Alexander Macrae emphasised the need for unity and education, and urged the continuation of the struggle; while chairman Donald Matheson re-affirmed the need for unity and active support for the efforts of the crofters' Members of Parliament. The Dornoch branch wished 'to draw special attention to the present destitute condition of this county, being chiefly owing to His Grace the Duke of Sutherland and other proprietors'. They did not accept that the recent rent-reductions came anywhere near to meeting the legitimate demands of the people, and resolved to agitate for change in 'the present oppressive land system'. In Durness the League demanded a proper and final settlement of the land question; and the Lochinver branch agreed to demand the restoration to the people of the deer forest of Glencanisp, 'where there is plenty of provision for ourselves and families. It extends twenty-one miles ... and is in the possession of an Englishman called Major Painter, while we at home are starving, and the land of our fathers lying waste'. Strathy, too, demanded redistribution of the land, as did the branches in Drumbeg, Achmelvich and Resolis, Assynt Central, Dornoch and Ferintosh and Culbokie; and at the social gathering of the Tongue branch, the chairman took the opportunity to advise those present to support the League more strongly than ever; for 'to the eye of the political seer' the future was 'pregnant with work, which required the most perfect co-operation'. That opinion was shared by the members of the branches at Tarbat, Skerray, Farr and Portskerra.

Not just in the far north, but throughout the country, the response to the election result was the same—a hardening of resolve on the part of the people. For although the landlords spoke of concession, they continued to conduct their affairs as before. The Duke of Westminster added ten thousand acres to his deer-forests, dispensing in the process with the services of two shepherds and their flocks, so that the deer might roam in peace. Near Strathpeffer, the Schoolbreds had leased extensive grazings, and were arranging to have the corries at the back of Ben Wyvis ploughed and sown for winter fodder, so that the hinds and the stags might be fat and fit for the following autumn, to afford better stalking and trophies for the sporting tenants. This latest development, the local League said, 'was proof (if such were needed) that our glens and straths admit of reclamation ... and must be for man and not for deer; and until this is fully secured, the ... agitation of the crofters must proceed unceasingly'. Crofters who petitioned the Duke of Sutherland for land to cultivate at Kildonan were told by his son, the Marquis of Stafford, that nothing could be done until his father came home. In fact the Duke was still not home by the end of the month, but in Jamaica, aboard his yacht the *Sans Peur* with some friends; they were in quarantine in Port Royal, yellow fever having been discovered aboard the vessel. But by that time a public meeting in the West Public School in Helmsdale had agreed that the Marquis' temporising answer was wholly unacceptable, and resolved to seize and cultivate the land forthwith.

But even though some contrived to ignore the passage of events, the landlords and their agents were under pressure, and many were concious of a real threat to the basis of their accustomed life-style. Even before the election, Munro Ferguson and other landlords' candidates had been compelled to issue statements on the land question so conciliatory that they found themselves under attack from their fellows for cravenly pandering to the ignorant masses. The Sutherlands' rent-reductions were now emulated by those of Lady Ross of Balnagown, in the district of Strathcarron, Kincardine and Ardgay. The defeated landlord-candidate for Ross-shire was soon to be consoled with the invitation to stand for Leith; and while that spring soliciting the candidature, he found time to address the Philosophic Institution on what he called the 'crofter problem', advocating a little less insecurity of tenure, a modicum of restraint by the owners of deer-forests, and the offer of forests and farms—for sale at market value of course—to the crofters. This view reflected landlord concession, however grudging; and even the *Scotsman* believed that the condition of some parts of the Highlands had become so serious 'that the urgency of the crofter question can hardly be exaggerated ... there are few questions more urgently calling for solution than the crofter question'.

In the same vein, the Marquis of Stafford announced that he would soon introduce to Parliament proposals for the 'amelioration' of the crofters' condition. The Land League, however, greeted the prospect with plain derision; the Crofters' Members rejected the proposals as worthless; and the pro-crofter press spoiled the Marquis' effect by publicising the fact that his parents' hungry and landless tenants were obliged to pay them rent for the privilege of searching their beaches and seashores for the mussels they used to bait their fish hooks. Meanwhile, the Marquis of Breadalbane, who owned around 200,000 acres, was assuring an audience in the Balmoral Hotel in Edinburgh of his hopes that any legislation on the land question would benefit crofters as well as landlords; his suggestion was that crofters be 'mixed-up' with the sheep-farmers, so that, as his Lordship confidently expected, 'the crofter would be a very great benefit to the farmer in supplying him with labour, and the farmer would be of considerable benefit to the crofter in giving him the means of earning a livelihood'. Munro Ferguson's speech to the Philosophic Institution had mingled a spirit of conciliation with undisguised fear of the result, should its proposals not be effected; to him, there was a need for 'some check' on the autonomous power of individual landlords, in view of the 'awful warning' of the Irish crofters' struggle; 'and it should be the endeavour of all to make any exertion or sacrifice to avert such calamities'.

At the same time, less conciliatory tones could still be heard. Lochiel feared 'legislation based on ignorance'; he still believed that the crofter movement 'owed its prominence largely to sentiment', and that security of tenure and fair rents were not in the crofters' interest. He longed for the day when people would get 'tired of listening to the flattering tales of professional agitators', and would return to their landlord. The Duke of Argyll had described the Napier Commission as 'little better than a great Shop of Scandal, in which every private spite could be indulged without immediate exposure, every unfounded conception of the past could be embodied in a narrative, and every myth could be represented as an historical truth'. Even now, in the spring of 1886, he was confident enough in his judgement and position to assure the public that any legislation to prevent the impoverishment of the crofters would be against the best interests of the Highlands—a view which represented, in the words of John Sturart Blackie, 'a masterly exposition of the economics of the Highland question from the point of view of the lords of the soil ... and those who take the Highlands as a field for mercantile speculation and pecuniary results'.

In his enthusiasm for 'progress', the Duke of Argyll was rivalled by his

The Marquis of Lorne, who said 'The Highlands can be rendered much more productive. Look at the progress made during the last century—is it not marvellous?'

son and heir, the Marquis of Lorne, who had lately returned from being Governor-General of Canada. At the beginning of January Lord Lorne addressed an audience of a thousand people in the Argyllshire Gathering Halls in Oban. He praised Lord Breadalbane as a true friend of the Oban Railway; he praised the initiative of railway companies in general, having encountered many fine examples in Canada; and most of all he praised progress itself, and the great principle of profit. He did not despair at all of the future of the Highlands, which he believed could be rendered much more productive. One had only to consider the progress made during the last century: was it not marvellous? The people of the Highlands were not deteriorated. They would never deteriorate either morally or physically. He had absolute faith in Highland honour.

Even as the Marquis spoke, however, events were taking place which he would surely have considered as a deterioration in the moral fibre of the crofting people. In Resolis, in the Black Isle, the tenantry of the Newhall estate attended a branch meeting of the Land League, at which they resolved not to pay their outstanding rents for the previous six months unless they were reduced by one third. They also voted unanimously to raise a legal fund for the defence of any members summonsed for rent-arrears, and to pay no rent at all, at least until they had next met together. In the preceding days, some of the people had received threatening notices relating to rent-arrears; the meeting, however, agreed to ignore those threats, and to withstand them united, should the need arise.

The Islands, too, had their share of confrontation and intransigence. Lady Gordon Cathcart wrote to the Lord Advocate in January, asking him to take punitive action against crofter insurrection. She thought it right to draw his attention, and the Government's, to the present state of her part of the Western Isles, where 'influences' had been at work— influences which had materially affected traditional relations between herself and her crofters, and which, if they were not checked, 'must lead to a very alarming state of matters'. Land League associations had been formed throughout the Hebrides. Land had been seized by force with threats of violence. Fences had been destroyed, and in South Uist the telegraph wires had been cut. Dangerous obstructions had been erected by night, even on the private road leading to Her Ladyship's own residence on the island. Moreover, the terrorism prevailing was such that the perpetrators of these crimes could not be discovered by the authorities, although well known; over the whole area, the rule of the law was 'practically in abeyance'.

That same month the War Office informed the Secretary of State that it would defer recalling the revolvers which had been transferred on loan to the police in the Highlands. Messrs Stuart, Rule and Burns of Inverness wrote to the Scottish Office, drawing the Secretary's attention to a cutting from the pages of the *Scottish Highlander*. It consisted of a letter from the poor crofters of Kintail, in which they pledged themselves to seize land needed to keep them from utter destitution. A few weeks later, the same solicitors sent a further cutting, which stated that the crofters on the

Kintail estate 'have carried out their resolution to take possession of the land'.

The day following the Marquis of Lorne's speech in the Argyllshire Gathering Hall, six girls from Uig, Lewis, were examined before Sheriff Black in Stornoway, and charged with participation in an assault on the shepherds of the large farmer of Linshader, during an attempt to place crofters' cattle on islands whose grazings they had previously enjoyed. Trouble was also reported in the parish of Lochs. For months conflict had simmered between the poor crofters of the district and the local large farmer, over the grazing of an island in nearby Loch Erisort. The previous summer the farmer had transported stock to this island, which the crofters believed to be theirs; and in December, just as the crofters of the district were voting Munro Ferguson out of office, one of the farmer's cows was found mysteriously drowned at the south end of the island. Prior to this, sheep had been disappearing so regularly that the survivors had already been removed to safer pasturage. Two days before Christmas the farmer visited the island itself, to find that another six cattle had vanished without trace. Then, on Christmas Day, yet another carcase was washed ashore at Bayble; and a few days later two more appeared on the shore at Lochs. The police were investigating the mystery, of course, but their lack of success only went to show that anti-landlord activity of this kind, if conducted with appropriate care, could be committed with impunity. This was true, whether it involved the destruction of peat-stack or of corn-stack, stone wall, fence, stock or crop, or whether it took the form of a rent-strike and refusal to remove. The message was clear, and fully understood from Argyll to the far north: organised agitation was safe and effective.

Not long before, Lord Lovat had complained bitterly that law enforcement no longer existed in the islands; that many lands had been seized by criminals, and were still in their possession; that rents were no longer paid, and that the forces of order were unable even to attempt the apprehension of any of the multitude of law-breakers at large. In places like Lewis, rent-strikes were now threatening to staunch the flow of income to the landlords' purses. In Skye, indeed, this had become a reality by the beginning of 1886. Early in the new year, Sheriff Ivory telegrammed the Scottish Secretary to report that, in the estimation of the procurator-fiscal in Portree, the crofters of Skye were now £17,000 in arrears. The MacDonald estate office had been reduced to asking crofters to pay whatever they felt they could afford; but nothing was paid, the crofters evidently believing they could not afford to pay even a penny in rent. Nor was this tactic confined to the MacDonald lands. During the first week of January the situation in Skye was the subject of very serious consideration by the Inverness-shire authorities. The recent attempted rent-collection had been a complete failure; for even the few crofters who might have been able to pay some rent had been deterred from doing so, 'either from fear of the Land League or from a wish to repudiate the landlords' right to rent'. Sheriff Ivory was in urgent communication with London again; to encourage his exertions, the landlords refused to pay their rates, with the result that both poverty relief and elementary education arrangements in the island were thrown in jeopardy. 'Matters are assuming a very serious aspect in the island', it was reported; 'no rent or taxes are being paid, and nothing can be done in the way of putting the law in force'. Nor could any sheriff-officer be got in the island to act in the recovery of rents; for 'the crofters will not pay a penny until they get their grievances adjusted'.

Still, the landlords sought an escape. Lord MacDonald's factor thought that while it was perfectly plain that a most serious crisis had arrived, the present state of matters simply could not endure. He believed that the crofters would like to pay their rents, and were only obstructed from so doing by the agitators who misled them. Similarly, Macleod of Macleod considered the success of the strike nothing short of a disgrace to the name of the island. He had heard reports that rent-arrears in Skye had reached £20,000; if that were true, he urged, then it was a measure of the extent to which the crofters had injured themselves, and alienated public sympathy for their cause. 'If they would listen to reason, they would see that if more land is what they want, the best way to get it is to pay for what they have'.

Understandably, this was not an argument that found favour among the crofters of Skye. When the Rates Committee and the Poor Board met in Portree in January, they had to consider the rates collector's report that letters of warning he had sent to the rent-striking crofters in Braes had been completely ignored, or else returned to him through the dead-letter office. Moreover, an official had been sent in person to Braes; he had called a meeting at the school-house there, inviting the people to come and pay what they owed; but only two had done so, and of the £119 due less than £2 had now been collected. To the chairman of the meeting, all this was most alarming; as were Lord MacDonald's decision to stop paying rates on his estate, and other, similar gestures throughout the island. Clearly, the matter must at once be reported to higher authority, and immediate steps would require to be taken. The chairman himself thought it quite reasonable for a landlord to withhold rates when his tenants paid no rents. However, the crofters of Skye were sure that such parity of treatment would not extend to the serving of decrees against Lord MacDonald, or the impounding of chattels from Armadale Castle in lieu of payment—for the chairman of the Skye Rates Committee was none other than Lord MacDonald's factor.

A few days after that meeting, the factor was writing again to the crofters, demanding the payment of rent, and reminding them that at the last rent-collection Lord MacDonald had authorised him to write-off one-half of the rise imposed in 1872, and to alter their rents accordingly. If they did not take advantage of this offer, he wrote, the rents would continue as they were at present; and, in the event of legal proceedings, 'the whole rent, as it at present stands, will be sued for with interest'. It would be evident to the crofters themselves, he added, 'that in not making payment of rents you are acting not only illegally, but also unfairly to Lord MacDonald'. That same week, the factor in Kilmuir was demanding the payment of rent; but only a handful of tenants paid, and then only a small portion of their due. In Dunvegan too, the rent-strike was reported to be solid and successful.

Not only were crofters' rents unpaid but even the big tenant-farmers were struggling to pay the rents for their sheep-farms. Only three years before, the Duke of Argyll had testified to 'the pleasure of dealing with capitalist farmers, who paid their thousands regularly as the dividends in the funds'. But now the profitability of the big farms had fallen dramatically, the farmers could no longer pay their rents, and the landlords were forced either to accept lower rents, or to take over sheep-farms which they could neither re-let nor run at a profit. In response to a petition from his tenant sheep-farmers, Lord MacDonald granted rent-reductions of up to a quarter, and regretted very much that, 'in the very trying circumstances in which he is placed at present, he cannot see his way to granting a greater abatement than he has allowed'. His farmers accepted the reductions, but only as a temporary measure, and were preparing to demand further reductions in rent; while the crofters, believing in the imminence of legislation to cancel all arrears of rent, simply payed none at all. The landlords found themselves in 'a situation of great uneasiness' which boded ill for all concerned, unless order was quickly and firmly reintroduced. However, the stage was now set at Westminster for the resolution of these uneasy circumstances.

For the London Government, showing greater detachment and wisdom than the Highland landlords, had realised the gravity of the situation, and had resolved, whether the landlords liked it or not, to invest with the power of the law some concessions to popular feeling in the Highlands. Accordingly, the Queen's Speech contained an intimation that a Bill would shortly be presented, with a view to 'mitigating the distressed condition of the poorer classes' in the Highlands. Within twenty-four hours the Marquis of Stafford had introduced his own Bill to the House, designed, he said, to 'make proper provisions for improving the condition of the crofters'. Given the uses to which the Marquis' family and agents had pressed the word 'improvement', and the innovations Sutherland had borne in its name, it is not surprising that his Lordship's Bill was unacceptable to all but his own sort, and was finally withdrawn. In February the Government introduced its own proposals. Mr Trevelyan believed that matters in the Highlands demanded the most serious attention, and that, as Secretary for Scotland, he could consent to delay no longer in dealing with these matters—not only for the sake of the crofters, but for the sake of the landlords besides. He hoped that 'Honourable Members will realise ... that we have come to a very serious stage of the question'.

All the Crofters' Members attacked the proposals which were then outlined. Donald MacFarlane was 'extremely disappointed' at this 'patchwork legislation'. Charles Cameron thought it illusory to expect such proposals as these to initiate a settlement of the question. Dr

Macdonald, it is true, thought that 'half a loaf is better than no bread'; but Mr Picton thought that 'the proposals of the Bill came nowhere near the indignation of the man proposing them'; and Dr Clarke felt bound to say of the Secretary's proposals that 'what he has given with one hand he has taken away with the other, and that is a proceeding which the hard-headed crofter will be well able to see through, and will refuse to accept as a settlement'.

Despite these complaints, however, the Bill received its First Reading in the Commons. When, in March, its proposals came before the House again for more detailed scrutiny, the criticisms were unchanged. Dr Macdonald reckoned that the Bill 'ignored what had been recommended; it recommended what had already been proved to have failed ... and it refused to recommend what had already succeeded'. Fraser-Mackintosh demanded more provision for the breaking up of the deer-forests, which were even then bringing in as much as £400,000 per year in sporting rents. The new Member for Wick, Macdonald-Cameron, in his maiden speech to the House, said he believed the Bill to be merely ameliorative. The new Member for Ross-shire thought it mere tinkering, and in need of much improvement. The landlords thought well of it, however; even the Marquis of Stafford thought it very fair in principle, though he did think that some Government assistance would be of great advantage to the impoverished fishermen of the northern coasts. No crofter missed the irony of his advocating the claims of these fishermen; for many of the inhabitants of the coastal villages had been moved there by 'improvements' on the Sutherland estates, with the assurance that their removal there would render them wealthy and thoroughly comfortable. The Member for Leeds Central—a man, it might be thought, with more experience of urban desolation than rural— thought the whole matter simply the result of the work of embittered agitators. Donald MacFarlane assured the House that the Bill, as presented, would be of practically no advantage to the Highland people; while as to being a settlement of the question, 'it was such a settlement as the old woman met when she tried to sweep back the sea with a broom. The wave of agitation was advancing, and would advance in spite of it'.

The Bill then went to its committee stage. Despite the determined efforts of the Crofters' Members, and despite Mackenzie's well-publicised contention that it was defective, and needed substantial alteration and improvement during its passage through the House, the Government had no intention of allowing its provisions to extend beyond the merely palliative. On the first Monday of April, while the Bill was still in committee, the Marquis of Stafford, mindful of the insecurity of his seat in the Commons, was urgently proposing amendments to it. Not one of these was of any real consequence; but he doubtless felt that it could be worth his seat in Parliament if he were able to demonstrate to people back in Sutherland that he had some concern for crofters' interests; certainly, he had no wish to emulate Munro Ferguson's loss of the Ross-shire seat. At

Skye crofter's son Dr R MacDonald, 'Crofters' Member' for Ross and Cromarty.

J MacDonald-Cameron, 'Crofters' Member' for Wick.

160

all events however, it was becoming clear that the Government intended to permit no substantial amendment to the Bill during its passage through Parliament. As the Member for Leeds Central had told the Commons during its second reading, the design of the Bill represented no more than a recognition that matters in the Highlands had reached a stage where 'it might be necessary to provide remedies which, even if in themselves not calculated to meet the needs of the people, would at least satisfy their imagination'.

The Bill passed from the Commons to the Lords. There, the Earl of Fife and the Duke of Argyll agreed that the whole crofting question had been sadly confused by 'appeals to class prejudice and popular ignorance'. According to Argyll, the Bill should be renamed the 'Bill to arrest agricultural improvements in the Highlands'; the popular mind had, in his view, been debauched—by the Irish example, by organised agitators, by the Napier Commission, and by decayed school-masters. Even Argyll, however, conceded that they were in a position that compelled them to agree to something being done; and he confessed that he would not vote against the Bill—not because he thought it was a good one, but on account of the position in which they were placed. Lord Abinger also spoke against the Bill, declaring himself aghast at the way it virtually expropriated landlords' private property without any compensation whatsoever. The Duke of Richmond, however, while insisting that he objected as strongly as anyone else to the provisions of the Bill, maintained that everyone present was aware in his heart that some such Bill was necessary. The Earl of Wemyss retorted that the whole notion of legislation in favour of the crofters involved 'a wrong and vicious principle', and called the Bill itself 'impolitic and mischievous'. Nevertheless, it was the views of Argyll and Richmond which carried the day; for the agitation in the north was now brisker than ever. Thus, the Bill was passed by the Lords and returned to the Commons, in a form substantially unchanged from the initial Government draft; and at the end of June, 1886, it received the Royal Assent, just one day before the dissolution of Parliament.

For the crofting people of the Highlands, it was a significant, though in many ways a partial, victory. The crofters themselves had been quick to spot the defects in the Government's proposals: towards the end of March, Sheriff Ivory passed on to the Scottish Secretary police reports from Skye which showed the crofters of Edinbane, Waternish and Kilmuir to be voicing dissatisfaction at the terms of the Bill. Moreover, Ivory reported, only one man had left Staffin for the Irish fishing, instead of the usual thirty; everyone was waiting to see the completed legislation, and was determined to agitate 'for more land than the Crofters' Bill proposes to give them'. Again, while the Bill was still in committee, a hundred and twenty crofters in Waternish had resolved that, unless it became law within the month, with amendments to meet their grievances, they would begin to cultivate the land 'wherever they found it suitable'. And at a League meeting in Barra in May, Michael Buchanan described the Bill as merely a step in the right direction: the agitation must continue, lest the landlords suddenly counter-attack.

Buchanan's analysis of the Bill was understandable; from the crofters' point of view it had been defective from the start. Yet it had survived the rigours of Westminster to become law. Not even the bitterest of the crofters' many enemies in the Lords had mustered the support necessary to sabotage it completely. True, there were attempts to baulk its provisions, defective as they were: Lord Lovat attempted to amend the Bill, so as to deny security of tenure to those crofters who went to the seasonal herring-fishing to earn the money with which to pay their rents; and, as Fraser-Mackintosh told the Commons in May, Lovat was also attempting to get all his crofters to sign a document leasing their holdings from him, before the Bill became law. The *Scottish Highlander* publicised this 'mean and contemptible' attempt to defeat the intentions of the Bill, and urged its readers on no account to take out such leases; for the effect of their doing so 'would be to exclude them from any benefits whatever under the Crofters' Bill'.

These manoeuvres, however, whether in Westminster or in Scotland, made little impact; for the truth of the matter was that the collective nerve of the Highland landlords had failed them. Admittedly, their prospects for the immediate future looked bleak; for events had disappointed their expectation that a general election would intervene before the Crofters' Bill could reach the Statute Book, allowing them, so they hoped, to reverse the defeats inflicted by the crofter-candidates at the previous election. Nor, indeed, was it clear that a further general election would result in the elimination of the Crofters' Members rather than the swelling of their ranks. The crofters' rent-strike, and a marked fall in the value of sheep-farm rents, were both having their effect on the landed purse. Worse still, perhaps, was the fall in the rental value of deer-forests: nearly one-half of all sporting estates in the Highlands were unlet, and it was increasingly hard even to sell them. In Aberdeenshire, estates to the value of one and a half million pounds were unlet; in Ross-shire the figure was a quarter of a million; and lands to the value of half a million pounds failed to find takers in each of the counties of Inverness, Caithness and Argyll. Above all, though, the realities of organised crofter resistence had finally got through to even the most anachronistic of the Highland proprietors.

This belated awakening corresponded to a coming of age within the crofters' movement itself: since the previous general election it had gained a new authority and vision, and was now judging the previous years of agitation and struggle as merely a preparatory engagement with the forces of landlordism. When it became clear that the Government had determined to allow no real concession to, and accept no radical amendment from, the Crofters' Members, there was no leader of the League, and perhaps no crofter in the Highlands, who saw the Bill as anything but the very first step towards the repossession of the land by the people. MacFarlane asserted in the Commons that lines of action had been arranged between the two front benches for the purpose of carrying the Bill in its original integrity; 'and I perceived that no amendment would be accepted by the Government from any quarter, especially from the representatives of those whom it was intended to benefit'. Few in the Highlands were unaware of this constraint, or could fail to draw the obvious conclusion from it.

Alexander Mackenzie (who, as a child on a Ross-shire croft, had had his ancient rifle sequestered by the factor, with the threat of his family's eviction, to keep him from poaching game) wrote that the new Act could only be accepted by the Highland people as a lever by which they might work out their freedom and gain permanent possession of the lands of their ancestors. For that purpose, it could be of considerable value; but he himself would not be satisfied until every inch of productive land in the Highlands had been placed at the disposal of those who were able and willing to till it. Until this was assured, the people must resolve to maintain 'the most persistent and determined agitation'; and if their 'resolute and comprehensive movement' should lead ultimately to the abolition of the sheep-farms, the deer-forests, the game-laws, even of the landlords themselves, then the latter had invited it. They had withstood the demands

Beaufort Castle, from which Lord Lovat wrote to Lord Lothian that, 'It is not the fixing of fair rents that raises so much objection...it is the entire destruction of trust and good feeling between landlord and tenant'.

Lord Lovat's tenants' houses in Bracara; 'Mr Fraser-Mackintosh has no stauncher supporters than the electors of North Morar and Bracara'.

of the people, and 'will only have themselves to blame. They are sowing the wind, and they will most assuredly reap the whirlwind'.

Emasculated and half-hearted though the Bill itself was, its introduction to Parliament, and its enactment in June, 1886, undoubtedly represented a tremendous achievement for the crofters. From the rich and the powerful, the common people of the Highlands had forced concessions to meet the grievances of generations, including security of tenure, compensation for improvement, the establishment of a land court, and the right to a judicially determined fair rent. No longer would the crofters face arbitrary and often brutal eviction, no longer could they be thrown physically from their homes, or driven out by threats of punishment, or cleared, by subtler means, from one part of an estate to the most unfavourable portions of the same estate. No longer would they face, to anything like the same extent, the horrors of deliberately imposed and implacably enforced impoverishment; for they were now—in theory at least—enabled to improve their holdings without thereby jeopardising their chances of remaining on them. Gone, too, were the visits of the landlord's rent-collector, the rack-renting and the debt-slavery which had characterised the Highland economy for generations, and had formed the obscene foundation of the splendour and extravagance indulged in alike by the descendants of clan chiefs and their southern-born imitators.

The reality, and the magnitude of the crofters' victory can be judged from the outraged reactions of the landlords and their protagonists. Fraser of Kilmuir saw the Bill as nothing more than 'the awful loom of future

164

communism;' and the pro-landlord press in general deemed it a frightful atrocity against the sacred rights of private landed property, and against all precepts of sound estate management. Such, however, was the strength of the movement by now that—collectivist atrocity or not—the proprietors could only complain, and intrigue to diminish the practical effects of the legislation.

A few weeks after the contents of the Bill became known, Lord Lovat wrote from Beaufort, on his elegant black-edged notepaper, to the Marquis of Lothian. He began by voicing the pious hope that 'the Government are not going to give in' on security of tenure to crofters, which would be 'most unfair to proprietors'. It was not the fixing of fair rents that raised so much objection, he went on (though the proposals to reduce rents in Skye were 'simple robbery'); ... 'It is the entire destruction of trust and good feeling between landlord and tenant'. Now, if Lord Lovat believed what he wrote—and, given the history of the Lovats, there might be more reason to trust him than there would some other proprietors— then he was remarkably naive in his conception of social relations then current in the Highlands. For by 1886, whatever 'trust and good feeling' might once have characterised landlords' relations with their inferiors had disappeared, along with the old clan society which the landowning chiefs themselves had done so much to destroy. Lovat's feelings, if they were as ingenuous as they appear, were by 1886 no more than misplaced and outdated sentiment; for whatever he, or indeed his own crofting tenants, thought of the matter, the consciousness of practically every proprietor and tenant in the Highlands contained less trust and good feeling than fear and contempt. Goodwill there might once have been towards landlords in general; and goodwill there had certainly once been towards certain individual landlords; but that popular goodwill had been outrageously abused and squandered by the landlords who took it as some divinely-bestowed birth-right; and though it had survived generations of that abuse, it had ceased to have practical significance by the 1880s, if not long before.

The significance of the 'Crofters' War' was, as much as anything, that it dispelled the myths by which the people of the Highlands had been held in subjection. In a sense its culmination, the Crofters' Act of 1886, was an anti-climax; for what Parliament now granted them they already had, the parliamentary concessions merely confirming them in what they had assumed during the course of the agitation of the previous years. And although Parliament had recognised their right to security of tenure, compensation, and fair fixed rents—concrete and tangible enough spoils in their own way—the central demand of the agitation, the delivery of the land to the people, was far from being granted.

Nevertheless, security of tenure provided the indispensible basis and starting-point for further agitation aimed at securing the ultimate objectives. In the days following the granting of the Royal Assent, the campaign continued unabated. From his terraced quarters in the shadow of Edinburgh Castle, Alexander Irvine, Sheriff of Argyll, was shortly to write to the Earl of Dalhousie, begging to report that in consequence of certain lawless acts by crofters, the Duke of Argyll had found it necessary to take out interdicts in the Court of Session. 'From the spirit of insubordination which has already been shown,' Sheriff Irvine wrote, 'there is reason to fear that the civil officers may be resisted and deforced ... My object in writing is to ask whether, in that case, I may trust to the help of a detachment of military in aid of the Civil Power.'

Although Dalhousie was to temporise then, merely instructing Irvine to keep him informed, the authorities had not seen the end of what the sheriff called the 'spirit of insubordination'. The forging and tempering of that spirit is the story of the Crofters' War. It won for the ordinary people of the Highlands what the *Oban Times* described—with magnificent élan—as 'an instalment of justice'. The struggle for the land was to continue—in a sense, indeed, it continues still. But the Crofters' Act of 1886 was a milestone in the long history of that struggle, and the agitation which led to it bears an enduring testimony to the truth of the old Gaelic proverb and cardinal slogan of the Highland Land League, *Is treasa tuath na tighearna*—'The people are mightier than a lord'.

Afterword

The 1886 Crofters' Act represented a remarkable victory for the Highland crofters. It was not an end, however, but a beginning. As all the crofters and their leaders knew, it was a grossly deficient piece of land legislation. Highland land agitation was to continue, albeit in a rather different form, until the end of the 1920s, by which time a series of legislative efforts had gone some way to removing many of the injustices of previous years. But the greatest single demand of the crofters' movement—the land to the people—was not met.

Nor has it yet been met. According to figures published recently, one tenth of one per cent of the Highland population own two thirds of the Highlands. Seventeen people, or companies, own seventy per cent of Caithness. Thirty-eight own eighty-four per cent of Sutherland. Seventy-six own eighty per cent of Ross-shire. And as John McEwan's *Who Owns Scotland?* makes clear, many of this tiny minority are descendants of the greatest enemies of the Land League. The Countess of Sutherland still owns 158,000 acres; Cameron of Lochiel owns 98,000. Lord Lovat has 76,000 acres; the Duke of Argyll has 74,000. Lord MacDonald still has 42,000, Macleod of Macleod 35,000; and the 34,000 acre estate of Novar is still today in the hands of the Munro Ferguson's of Novar.

That the people who live and work on this land still do not own the land and still do not control the land is not, however, a matter for which the men and women of the land agitation of the 1880s bear responsibility.

Further reading and some sources

On the land agitation and its wider historical context, there are five classes of sources.

Modern Printed Sources

Of the many books which concern themselves with the Highlands in the century and a half after Culloden, James Hunter's *The Making of the Crofting Community* (John Donald 1976) is without equal, and is essential reading. Well-referenced and with a comprehensive bibliography, it is the only modern work which really explains what was happening in the nineteenth century Highlands. It includes two chapters on the land agitation up to 1886. No other author on the nineteenth century Highlands perceives and takes as the starting point of his analysis the fact that the central problem was not a 'crofter problem' but a 'landlord problem'.

No book has ever taken the land agitation as its principal subject; J Cameron's *The Old and the New Highlands and Hebrides* (Kirkcaldy 1912), which covers the agitation at some length, is neither accurate nor useful. A number of articles on the subject have appeared in recent decades in specialised journals; note especially those by Kellas *(History Today 1962)*, Crowley *(Scottish Historical Review, 1956)* and Hanham *(Transactions of the Royal Historical Society, 1969)*. There is a chapter on the subject in J Dunbabin's *Rural Discontent in 19th century Britain* (Faber, 1974). The two chapters in Hunter's book, however, are better than any of these, and should be read in conjunction with his articles in *Northern Scotland* (1973), and *Scottish Historical Review* (1974). See also, Donald Meek, Gaelic Poets of the Land Agitation in the *Transactions of the Gaelic Society of Inverness, XLIX*.

The lack of modern printed material on the anti-landlord mass-movement of the 1880s reflects the predisposition of those historians who have concerned themselves with the Highlands. Their failure— with the main exception of Hunter—to recognise the landlord problem as the *key* to nineteenth century Highland affairs has resulted in a mass of implicitly and explicitly anti-crofter material. Two examples are especially noteworthy. Philip Gaskell's study of Morvern deformed by nineteenth century Highland landlordism, *Morvern Transformed* (Cambridge University Press, 1968), and David Turnock's article 'North Morar: The Improvement Movement on a West Highland Estate' *(Scottish Geographical Magazine, 1969)* will both repay careful scrutiny as excellent examples of how not to interpret the evidence for Highland history in this period.

Contemporary Printed Sources

The Duke of Argyll presented the landlord view of 'improvement' in his *Crofts and Farms in the Hebrides* (Edinburgh, 1883). J S Blackie expounded the pro-crofter viewpoint in *Gaelic Societies, Highland*

Depopulation and Land Law Reform. (Edinburgh, 1880), and in *The Scottish Highlanders and the Land Laws* (London, 1885). See also G B Clark, *The Highland Land Question* (London, 1885); D H MacFarlane, *The Highland Crofters versus Large Farms* (London, 1884); and J MacLeod, *Highland Heroes of the Land Reform Movement* (Inverness, 1917).

Contemporary Newspapers and Journals

The London *Times* reported extensively on the agitation and has the advantage, for the researcher, of being indexed. The *Glasgow Herald,* the *North British Daily Mail,* and the *Scotsman* all carried long reports; while the second was pro-crofter, the last was violently anti-crofter. The Highlands of the 1880s supported many local newspapers. Most of them were anti-crofter; but the *Oban Times* and the *Invergordon Times* provided excellent coverage from a strongly pro-crofter viewpoint. Alexander Mackenzie's *Celtic Magazine* reported extensively on the League and the agitation, with valuable comment and penetrating analysis. John Murdoch's *Highlander* is essential for the early years of the agitation, and Mackenzie's *Scottish Highlander* for the later years.

Official Publications

Hansard's *Parliamentary Debates* gives a fine insight into the thinking and attitudes of the ruling-class with reference to the Highlands. The Report and four volumes of Evidence arising from the Napier Commission is the single most important publication for the history of the nineteenth century Highlands. Officially entitled *The Report of the Commissioners of Inquiry into the Condition of the Crofters and Cottars in the Highlands and Islands of Scotland* (1884), it is a mine of information on the Clearances period and on the early years of the agitation. Much valuable information is contained in more specialised sources such as, for example, *Return of Agrarian Offences committed in Crofting Parishes, Scotland (1874-1888)* (1888, LXXXII), and *Papers Relating to the Despatch of Government Force to Skye* (1884-85, LXIV).

Unpublished Papers and Records

Two valuable sources are the J S Blackie Papers in the National Library of Scotland, and John Murdoch's longhand autobiography in the Mitchell Library. A convenient entrée to material held by the Scottish Records Office is provided by two publications of the Scottish Record Office, *The Highlands and Islands. Summary List of Material in the Scottish Records Office relating to the history of the Highlands and Islands,* and, *Sources for Crofting Disturbances, c 1883-6* (Ex H/378).

The following items are of particular interest: AF50, Records of the Royal Commission on the Highlands and Islands, 1883; HHI, Scottish Office Miscellaneous Files from 1885, especially HHI/842, Confidential mission of inquiry by Mr Malcolm McNeill on behalf of the Secretary of

Scotland 1886-7. Among the Lord Advocate's Papers, Box Two contains excellent source material on the agitation. The Lothian Muniments, (GD40), also preserve much information on the agitation: see, for example, GD40/16/3 (Lady Gordon Cathcart on law and order); GD40/16/33 (Lord Lovat on the Skye rent-reductions and 'simple robbery'); GD40/16/32 (the report of McNeill's secret mission in the Highlands). Finally, the Sheriff Ivory papers (GD1/36) contain a most important body of documents on the agitation, with reference to Skye.